Saving Upper Newport Bay

Saving Upper Newport Bay

How Frank and Frances Robinson Fought to
Preserve One of California's Last Estuaries

Cassandra Radcliff

Top Reads Publishing, LLC

Vista, California

First Edition

ISBN: 978-1-970107-11-1 (paperback)

Library of Congress Control Number: 2019915554

Saving Upper Newport Bay: How Frank and Frances Robinson Fought to Preserve One of California's Last Estuaries is published by:
Top Reads Publishing, LLC
1035 E. Vista Way, Suite 205, Vista, CA, 92084-4213 USA

For information please direct emails to:
teri@topreadspublishing.com

Cover artwork: "Morning Marine Layer–Back Bay Newport Beach" by Terry Ann Stanley, terrystanleyart.com
Cover design: Teri Rider
Book layout and typography: Teri Rider & Associates

Printed in the United States of America on recycled paper

Dedication

This book was made possible by a generous grant from the Keating family in honor of their father, Jack Keating.

Saving Upper Newport Bay is dedicated to Frank and Frances Robinson, and those who tirelessly volunteered or donated their money alongside them. It is also dedicated to the past, current, and future volunteers who continue the Robinsons' legacy.

"Never doubt that a small group of thoughtful, committed citizens can change the world. Indeed, it is the only thing that ever has."

— Margaret Mead

Contents

Foreword

BY JACK KEATING

PRESIDENT OF THE UPPER NEWPORT BAY NATURALISTS FROM 1993-1999 AND
PRESIDENT OF NEWPORT BAY NATURALISTS AND FRIENDS FROM 2001-2004

When I was asked to write a foreword for this book on the saving of the bay, I couldn't have been more delighted. It gives me the opportunity to put into writing my appreciation for the years of effort that went into the original citizens' campaign and the absolutely crucial leadership role played by Frank and Frances Robinson. The book also presents an opportunity to recognize the contribution of the many unsung heroes whose dedication has enabled the bay to survive and thrive over the subsequent 50 years.

Looking back over the history of the decades-long campaign is a reminder of how success takes sustained dedication from many individuals working on many connected but different tracks. In this case, it took a personal intervention by the Robinsons, a willingness to pursue many challenges over many years, and success in engaging the community. Frank and Frances proved adept at enlisting the support of individuals with the needed legal, conservation, and planning expertise.

By the time I became personally involved, the legal battle had been fought and won, but—as Frank himself noted—that was really the start of the work. Protecting a wild place such as the Upper Newport Bay in a heavily urbanized setting needs constant attention, both vigilance and hands-on involvement.

In our case, the California Department of Fish and Wildlife and Orange County Harbors, Beaches and Parks created a platform for community involvement via the creation of a training program to equip members of the public to be effective stewards of the bay. I was a member of the first naturalist graduating class in 1990. One of the particular successes in our case was the willingness of the Friends and the Naturalists to share the space, and merge to form the Newport Bay Naturalists and Friends 10 years later. As president of the Naturalists, I worked closely with Lane Koluvek, long-term president of the Friends to integrate the two nonprofits; an undertaking that always requires good will and a shared focus on the "big picture."

The story of how the bay was preserved as one of the few remaining coastal wetlands in Southern California is a testament to what can be achieved when a community puts its mind to it. I am proud to have been able to play a part in producing today's vibrant Newport Bay Conservancy with 200 active volunteers running educational programs, doing habitat restoration, and providing docent and concierge services to the public. I hope this book will help to inspire and encourage the next generation.

John ("Jack") Keating

A History of Human Influence on the Bay

People have lived in California for 10,000 years. Native American, Spanish, Mexican, and American cultures have all called the Newport Bay area home.

Native Americans

The earliest humans lived in the bay 9,000 years ago. Nearly 2,000 years ago, Native Americans lived in villages along the shores of Upper Newport Bay. They thrived eating the waterfowl, fish, shellfish, and plants found there, but, as with many Native American nations, they largely disappeared within 50 years of the Mission Period.

The Spanish Mission Period

In the late 1700s through the early 1800s, Spanish missionaries built 21 missions from San Diego to Sonoma, the closest to Newport Beach being Mission San Juan Capistrano. The Spanish called the bay *Bolsa de Gengara*, meaning "bay with high banks."

Sepúlveda's Rancho

After Mexico won independence from Spain in 1821, the area around Upper Newport Bay became known as Bolsa de San Joaquin. The flamboyant Don José Antonio Andrés Sepúlveda owned Rancho San Joaquin, a 48,000-acre ranch with a hacienda on what is now the Rancho San Joaquin Golf Course. Sepúlveda made his fortune selling beef during the Gold Rush. But years later, the boom of the Gold Rush had ended, a major drought had devastated his grazing land, and he had gambled away too much of his money. These were a few of the reasons why Sepúlveda decided to sell his land at a reduced price to James Irvine I and his partners.

James Irvine's Ranch

The United States acquired California and other lands from Mexico after the Mexican-American War, and California gained statehood in 1850. When James Irvine purchased the land from Sepúlveda in

1864, he paid just 36 cents an acre. He used his 101,026 acres of land in Orange County to raise sheep to produce wool. Like Sepúlveda, he built a house on what is now the Rancho San Joaquin Golf Course.

The Dream of a Great Port

A small paddle-wheeled steamboat called *Vaquero* is the reason for the area's current name of Newport. In 1870, it carried a load of lumber into the bay, making the stop a "new port." In the 1880s, two brothers, James and Robert McFadden, dreamed of making the bay into a great industrial port. Their dreams were never realized due to the ever-shifting sandbar at the harbor's entrance and the fact that Irvine refused to grant Southern Pacific Railroad a right-of-way across his ranch to the harbor.

Commercial Salt Works

In 1934, dikes and evaporating ponds were built in the upper reaches of the bay to harvest salt to sell to commercial laundries, water softener concerns, and other customers. The salt works harvested 5,000 tons of salt per year. The operation was abandoned after flooding in 1969 severely damaged the ponds and washed away the salt (a flood in 1938 ruined that annual harvest, as well). Today the only remaining evidence of the salt works are two strips of land (remnants of the former salt dikes) near Jamboree Bridge.

Shellmaker Island Calcium Supplement Production

Shellmaker Island, which is actually a peninsula, was dredged for ancient shell deposits for use as a calcium supplement in chicken feed from 1939 to the late 1980s. The operation could produce 1,200 tons of the supplement per month, but because the land became part of the Upper Newport Bay Ecological Reserve, the Shellmaker Dredging Company was unable to renew its lease on the land in the 1980s.

Suburban Population Boom

Orange County was one of the fastest-growing communities in the United States from the 1950s to 1970s, largely in part to the area's booming aerospace industry. The population grew from 216,000 people in 1950 to 1,420,000 in 1970. Even the number of boats more than doubled in 10 years, going from 14,000 in 1960 to 34,000 in 1970. With the number of residents and boats soaring, developers like The Irvine Company had a lot of business.

Preface

The Beginning

～⁓

It took 14-year-old Jay Robinson less than five minutes to ride his bike down the hill to North Star Beach. It was the summer of 1963, and his mother had told him to go play outside. The year before, Jay, his little sister, and his parents moved from La Cañada to Newport Beach's Westcliff neighborhood. Their new home was just two blocks away from Upper Newport Bay.

The bay was Jay's playground. Kids in the neighborhood could bicycle along the high bluffs or hike the dirt paths down to the water. There they could play on the sandy beach and watch for jumping fish, crabs scuttling around on the shore, and birds dive-bombing into the water for a meal. And if their parents had instructed them to, they would dig into the mud to harvest fresh chione clams for that night's dinner.

Just south of North Star Beach was noisy construction on the new Dover Shores community, which was nearly completed. Farther south was the lower bay, a private marina with plenty of boats, which were often whizzing around towing water-skiers behind them, as they also did in the upper bay. The houses in the lower bay were upscale estates with manicured lawns, palm trees, private docks, and personal yachts, unlike the Robinsons' more modest home. Beyond the marina, at the bay's mouth, was Balboa Peninsula and Balboa Island. Kids just a few years older than Jay were celebrating summer by swimming in the Pacific Ocean all day and dancing at ocean-front Rendezvous Ballroom all night.

Just north of North Star Beach stood a 100-foot-tall white cliff jutting out into the water. Beyond that was another mile of the bay's water channel, Middle Island, Upper Island, and acres of marshlands.

The salt marshes flooded during the twice-a-day high tides, and the freshwater marshes filled when rainwater flowed from inland Orange County. The Western Salt Company was located at the uppermost reaches of the bay. Its 5,000 tons of collected salt was drying in the hot summer sun before it could be harvested.

Across from North Star Beach was the shore of the low-lying Shellmaker Island. The island had been dredged for shell deposits for use in chicken feed since 1939, and even on that day in 1963, the shell processing plant puffed away, pumping smoke and dust into the air. Just beyond Shellmaker, cars drove on the narrow two-lane road called Back Bay Drive, with southbound travelers heading to Balboa Island.

This view is what Jay would have seen on that summer day in 1963, after reaching North Star Beach, if he had been able to drop his bike in the sand, remove his shoes, and dip his feet into the cool, calm water. But the young teenager was stopped before he could access the beach by a sign on a wooden stake. It read:

PRIVATE PROPERTY
Closed to all unauthorized persons
Violators will be prosecuted
CPC 602

Below that was "The Irvine Company."

In the middle of a citrus orchard off Irvine Boulevard in Tustin, a small stucco building near the old Irvine family home served as the headquarters of The Irvine Company. Charles S. Thomas became the company's president in 1960, when there were just 10 staff members. During his time there, Thomas had seen potential in an engineer named William Mason, whom he made vice president of engineering, and Raymond Watson, whom he made vice president of planning. These three men would run the company as president, in turn, for the coming 14 years.

The men in the office were discussing several plans for new communities in Orange County. The county's population had tripled in the past decade, growing from 216,000 people in 1950 to 704,000 in 1960. Proper planning was needed so new residents could live, work, shop, and recreate.

The small team was hard at work. They were preparing a University Community plan, which they would submit to the Orange County Board of Supervisors for approval the following year. The Dover Shores community was almost completed, and the Board of Supervisors had approved the plan they submitted in May to develop Upper Newport Bay into a pleasure harbor, just as the lower bay had been. Signs had just gone up around the bay declaring the land was private property, as dredging and bulldozing would soon begin.

The Irvine Company had been working on the idea of a pleasure harbor in the upper bay since the early 1940s; they would build a water ski basin, a marine stadium and rowing course, boat basins, docks, fueling stations, and commercial strips along the banks.

The problem was, The Irvine Company did not own all the land in the bay.

With the recently approved plan, however, The Irvine Company and the County of Orange agreed to trade land so the harbor could finally be built. The Irvine Company would receive 157.1 acres in Upper Newport Bay, and the county would receive 450.3 acres of Irvine-owned land elsewhere. Everyone involved felt good about the deal, the consensus being it would be a big money-maker for both the company and the county. The Board of Supervisors, Charles S. Thomas, and his small staff were pleased it was finally going to happen… or so they thought.

Part One | Protest

Chapter One

SELFISH REASONS

~∘~

At 1007 Nottingham Road, 45-year-old Frances Robinson—known as "Fran" by friends and family—was enjoying a quiet summer day. Born and raised in Los Angeles, Frances was a well-educated woman who attended L.A. City College and the University of California, Berkeley. When she lived in the San Gabriel Valley, she served as president of the La Cañada Child Guidance Clinic and the San Gabriel Valley Child Guidance Clinic. In sixth grade her teacher had suggested that she'd be a good class secretary, but Frances responded, "No, Miss Irvin, I'm planning to run for president." She ran for class president and won, of course.

In 1963 here in Orange County, life had slowed down a bit for Frances. She was no longer a president, but a mother of two and housewife—and on this summer day she was enjoying the quiet of her Newport Beach home. Her husband, Frank, was at work; her son, Jay, was bicycling around the bay; and her daughter, Dana, was playing with the neighborhood girls. Fran was likely organizing her paper clippings, writing a letter, tending her showcase garden, or swimming laps in her pool. She loved the water and swam every day, and even though she was never very good at it, she loved to water ski in the bay, and occasionally on Lake Powell during vacations.

Fran tried to give her kids what her mother gave her. Her mother worked five and a half days a week but would always take her to do something fun on the weekend. Fran loved taking the Red Car, an electrical rail network, around Los Angeles, visiting the L. A. Museum of Natural History or the beach. Her mother also took her to political rallies and candidates' forums, which led to Fran's interest in community involvement. But the greatest joy of her life, Fran thought, was being taken to the beach when she was a kid. She and her mother would arrive no later than 6 a.m., before there were any other footprints there, and swim among the seaweed. That's why Fran and her husband had moved to this Westcliff neighborhood, so their kids could play in the water just as Fran had.

Her son, Jay, had come back home sooner than expected, and interrupted her quiet summer day. He told her something she found very distressing: there was a sign on North Star Beach that read "Private Property."

When Frank arrived home and they told him the news, he was upset too. The family set out toward the bay, with Jay leading his parents and Dana down to the sign at North Star Beach. "We walked down," Fran said, "and found that 'private beach' signs [had] been posted in four areas along the bay."

Fran, who collected newspaper clippings on topics that interested her, easily found a recent article about a proposed land swap between the county and The Irvine Company. "I'd taken political science courses in college," she said, "and I'd learned that everyone has the right to use the water up to the mean [high] tide line."

Frances thought they could fight this and keep the beaches public for everyone to use.

———

With their son's discovery in 1963, Fran's quiet life in Newport Beach ended abruptly, and things began moving at a rapid pace. Walls had gone up around the private areas seemingly overnight, and fill dirt had already been dumped on top of the sandy beaches. "The public [was] shut off completely from this waterfront," Fran said.

At this time, Frank and Fran had no particular interest in the ecology and environmental importance of the bay. Their motive was to save it for the residents who had been using it and the future generations who would suffer from the loss of access. In fact, a lot of California residents were thinking this way in the 1960s. One 1968 Council for Planning and Conservation (CPC) newsletter demonstrates that public access was a concern up and down the coast. "Strong citizen concern over beach access has been expressed to the CPC particularly by surfers," it read, "who have become experts on their diminishing access to coastline." One surfer in the military wrote to them, saying, "By the time I return to California, my daughter will be old enough to swim. I hope I won't be forced—by beaches being closed to the public—to teach her in a pool."

Even though things were moving at lightning speed, Fran was more than able—and more than willing—to work quickly. Twelve years before, she'd taken 2-year-old Jay to her favorite beach, Zuma Beach in Malibu, only to find a private property sign denying them access to the water. "I was mad," she said. She told herself, "If I ever live where I see this happening, I will do something." This, right now, was her time to do something. Fran, who was ready, organized, eloquent, intelligent, and determined, moved fast to catch up and hopefully get ahead of The Irvine Company's construction.

Fran's first order of business was to sit down at her typewriter and write a letter to the Orange County Board of Supervisors. She sent it to others, including the editor of the local paper, the *Daily Pilot*. Fran would write many letters in the coming years, and there is no doubt that her congenial, well-written letters were a major player in the battle to save the bay. This first letter, dated August 22, 1963, is printed here in its entirety. It read:

> When we purchased our home on Nottingham Road in Westcliff, after a search of several months, a major reason for our choice of location was the fact that just a very short walk down the hill were some small but delightful 'Back Bay' beaches.
>
> Several weeks ago, our son came home with the distressing news that 'private beach' signs had been erected on <u>all</u> the beaches. These are in the Dover Shores development. We walked down and checked and found that 'private beach' signs had been posted in four areas along the bay, on Polaris Drive, roughly between Nottingham Road and Westcliff Drive. Wherever on the water there wasn't a house being built, there was a 'private beach' sign.

Walls have gone up around these 'private beaches,' and fill dirt is being dumped on top of the largest beautiful sandy beach. <u>The public is being shut off completely from this waterfront!</u>

Does this represent the tidelands acreage to which The Irvine Company asks full title in exchange for other acreage farther back on the bay? According to an article in the August 14 edition of the *Daily Pilot*, 'the county gives to Irvine 114 acres of filled tidelands, free of public rights for fishing, navigation and commerce...'

If the Dover Shores 'private' beaches are part of this 114 acres, we protest.

We think the giving of land by The Irvine Company for the creation of a park is commendable. Certainly Newport Beach has a dearth of such facilities. However, we doubt that the value of the lands offered, though larger, would equal the value of the lands near our home which lie near the entrance to the 'Back Bay' and immediately across from the Dunes and the Newporter Inn.

It is surely in the public interest to have the parks which we understand are planned both at 23rd St. and at the extreme end of the bay.

It certainly is also in the interests of those who live in the areas bordering the new Dover Shores community to continue to have access to <u>at least one</u> of the beach areas immediately adjacent to our homes. To our knowledge, there is no comparable sandy beach anywhere along the bay.

We cannot speak for other residents of Westcliff, since we haven't discussed the matter with them. We can, however, speak for our child and her playmates on this street who very frequently have used the beaches which now display the 'private' signs.

Are you aware that many people go there to fish?—that the largest beach (which we pointed out is being covered with fill dirt) is a favorite secluded spot for picnickers?—that children adore collecting shells there? Is this lovely area to be 100 percent denied to every family who can't afford a costly Dover Shores home?

Parks have been promised for a future day at a greater distance from our home; and meanwhile, our children are deprived of playing on the beach which is almost in our backyard.

By all means, let the purchasers of property in Dover Shores have their private beach. The area is beautiful and will be a credit to Newport.

However, we think it is mandatory that one of the beaches, preferably the largest one, remain fully accessible to all the people of our area and to anyone else who cares to use it.

The letter was signed Mr. and Mrs. J. Frank Robinson.

While The Irvine Company's bulldozers moved quickly, the Robinson family moved even more quickly. Within days of Jay's discovery of the North Star Beach sign, the Robinsons went door to door to collect signatures of neighbors who also wanted to protect the bay. Within two weeks, on August 29, Fran's letter ran in the paper. On October 1, 1963, the Robinsons submitted a petition with 200 signatures to request that county supervisors put a hold on the land trade, which was crucial to the marina's development.

———

The people on the south side of the bay had their own reasons to oppose The Irvine Company's development plan. Two months after the Robinsons formally submitted their petition, the Newport Beach City Council expressed its own displeasure with the plan during a city council meeting. According to the December 4, 1963 issue of the *Daily Pilot,* the council took issue with the proposed alteration of Back Bay Drive. The scenic road was constructed from 1900 to 1920 along the opposite side of the bay from the Robinsons' home and North Star Beach. The narrow road ran between the saltmarshes and the tall cliffs, giving access to the salt dikes, the Shellmaker Island dredging operation, and other parts of Newport Beach.

The Irvine Company planned to re-route a 1,800-foot section of the scenic roadway to a higher elevation and put buildings where the road had been. At that December city council meeting, council members Donald Elder and Dee Cook said alteration of the scenic road was "becoming a controversial subject" and that concerned citizens were sending letters asking them to preserve the road's "incomparable view."

While The Irvine Company insisted the new route would offer an even more scenic view of the upper bay, the city council was not swayed. Elder criticized the maps The Irvine Company used to illustrate the new route, saying they looked like "drawings my young son could do." (This was the first time the company was accused of using bad maps, but it wasn't the last.)

Mayor Charles E. Hart told The Irvine Company, "We'll be reasonable. The Bayside Drive location is now the only roadblock in your plans."

The city council unanimously opposed The Irvine Company's plan—for now. Even though access to North Star Beach wasn't the reason for the opposition, development still was stalled for a time. Frank and Fran would use this time to prepare to block the revised Irvine development proposal.

What They Didn't Know Yet

In the early 1960s, when the Robinsons moved to Newport Beach, Upper Newport Bay was one of the largest remaining estuaries in Southern California with a total size of approximately 1,000 acres. But Frank and Fran's motive to get involved was not environmental. They only knew they wanted their children to grow up playing in the water, just as Fran had when she was a kid growing up in Los Angeles.

"It was all selfish in the beginning," said Frank. "They were going to dredge out and narrow the channel and make it like lower Newport Bay. We got a little upset."

Their fight began as a simple objection to restricting public access to the bay. But as time went on and as they learned more about the bay, they began to realize the rare treasure they had in their own backyard. Frank said, "As we got into it, it was a little bigger than a bellyache about not having a beach for our kids."

As the Robinsons would later learn, Upper Newport Bay is the only place left in Southern California that still has all the habitat types of a complete coastal wetlands system. It is home to the richest diversity of birds and fish in Southern California, including five rare or endangered bird species.

〜〜〜〜〜〜〜〜〜 Aerospace Connections 〜〜〜〜〜〜〜〜〜

Frank Robinson worked at Autonetics, a division of North American Aviation, which became a part of Rockwell and is now a part of Boeing. North American Aviation developed navigation systems for ships, submarines, missiles, aircraft, and spacecraft, and at its height employed 36,000 people on its 188-acre Anaheim campus.

Frank's biggest contribution at work was his patented ball bearing design. Because his ball bearings outlasted those of MIT, the United States Air Force gave Autonetics its business. Frank was so valued at Autonetics that the company supported him, letting him make bay-related phone calls at work and take time off to fight for the bay. "I took an awful lot of time off from work," Frank said. "The company was great because they encouraged people to participate in civic activity."

What Frank did for the bay, he said, was "a reflection of what I did in my professional career. Engineering demands that you finish something or have nothing. There are a lot of great starters in the world… But the ability to finish something, particularly when it gets tiresome, boring, and you get into the grind of writing reports, had a lot to do with how I conducted my kind of environmental business."

It was through work that Frank met Allan Beek and Charles Greening. Later in life, Frank met Jack Keating, a retired aerospace engineer who also lived in Newport Beach. All four men played a huge part in protecting Upper Newport Bay.

Allan Beek

Computer hardware engineer at Autonetics

How he helped the bay: Allan Beek formed the nonprofit foundation Orange County Foundation for the Preservation of Public Property to raise funds for legal expenses. During four years of the legal fight, the nonprofit raised about $40,000, mainly from small donations from hundreds of individuals.

A lifelong resident of Newport Beach, Allan carpooled or rode the bus with Frank Robinson to work. "Frank liked to talk a lot," Allan said. "I think that part of his success was that he spent half the day on the telephone." Frank liked to talk so much that when they rode the bus together, Allan said, "I'd sometimes be trying to read my *Scientific American*. Frank would like to talk, so I would read while he talked!"

Dr. Charles ("Chuck") Greening

Head of Human Factors Research at Autonetics

How he helped the bay: Chuck Greening was a trustee for the Orange County Foundation for the Preservation of Public Property, president of the Friends of Newport Bay for eight years, served on the board for more than 20 years, and manned the "Bird Stop" on the Friends Tours.

After working for the Manhattan Project during WWII, Chuck Greening helped improve aircraft equipment and design intuitive training programs and procedures at Autonetics. Chuck said, "I have never seen anyone work so long and hard and intensively for a cause as the Robinsons, both of them, Frank and Fran."

Jack Keating

Aerospace Engineer at Douglas Aircraft Company (later McDonnell Douglas)

How he helped the bay: Jack Keating served as president of the Upper Newport Bay Naturalists and then Newport Bay Naturalists and Friends for 10 years.

After retiring, Jack Keating brought the project management and people management skills he learned at Douglas to the fight for the bay. "My only experience had been with the federal government in aerospace," he said. "But I was able to build relationships with the key people at different agencies and was able to get us moving in the same direction without stepping on too many land mines."

The more Jack thought about nature, the more interesting it became. "The natural system is so much more complex than a rocket," he said. "There are so many variables in nature. A rocket will either do what it's supposed to do or fail. Nature adapts and changes." He was familiar with missile control systems and propulsion systems from work, but he realized he wanted to learn "about the natural systems and how various animals and organisms interact to produce a successful result, which is life."

Chapter Two

A Bad Deal

───⌁───

In 1964, six months after Frances wrote to Jesse Unruh, head of the State Tidelands Committee, she got a response. Unruh would send one of his assistants, Charles Baldwin, down from Sacramento to visit with the Robinsons. "We set up an appointment, and he came down," Fran said.

When Baldwin knocked on the door of 1007 Nottingham Road, Frances answered to find a totally bald, imposing young man. "There were about 40 of us in the living room," Frank said. A group had gathered to show Baldwin the information they had collected about the trade.

In February, the city of Newport Beach and The Irvine Company had reached an agreement. The decision went to the board of supervisors for approval that March. The revised plan included a 4.5-acre city beach below West Bluff with 650 feet of water frontage and room for parking and pedestrian access. (The city had previously demanded two parks below West Bluff.) There would be acreage for an Orange County regional park at the mouth of Big Canyon and East Bluff. And the scenic shoreline along Back Bay Drive would be retained, although some of the road could be realigned.

Since they had petitioned to stall the trade, the Robinsons and their small group of supporters had begun doing extensive research. Frank said, "We realized this was not a 'NIMBY' [not in my backyard] thing, like somebody cutting off your view or messing up your backyard… It took a lot of reading and education on our part."

"We developed one hell of a network of helpers that had priceless information," Frank said. "I would pick up the phone and talk to somebody, [and] in the mail the next day, I'd get something that might have taken me a month to dig out." A retired businessman from the neighborhood, George Friedl, Jr., helped a lot. Frances said Friedl was "a brilliant researcher, a brilliant man, and he'd done most of the initial research that we were not qualified to do." Frances also said there were a lot of local government employees who wanted to help but didn't want to lose their jobs. There were "four people on the staff of the Board of Supervisors who were willing to help us because they thought that what we were doing was the right thing."

"This land trade was the most complicated documentation," Frank said in a 1992 interview with oral historian James A. Aldridge. "You cannot trust any documents. You have to dig them all out and find the weaknesses in them." That's because The Irvine Company, according to Frank, often misrepresented the facts. "Irvine was presenting selective information," Frank said. "There was misrepresentation of their rights in the upper bay; not an outright lie, but not the full truth either… I found this to be a very common pattern."

After Charles Baldwin spoke with the group gathered in the Robinsons' living room and received a personal tour of the bay, he left with boxes and boxes of documents in his car and drove back to Sacramento. He reviewed the maps, tax records, photographs of the bay, and other documents, then called the Robinsons and said, "It's one of the worst rip-offs of public land I have ever seen."

A Possibly Illegal Exchange

Fran had remembered correctly what she learned in her college political science class; everyone does have the right to use the water up to the mean high tide line. Public access to tidelands for commercial uses like fishing and shipping was so vital to civilization that these lands have been protected by law as far back as the 6th century. This concept can be found in the Magna Carta, the United States Constitution, and even in the Constitution of the State of California.

Ownership and development rights were more complicated than the Robinsons could have imagined. The laws were so obscure, in fact, that the Robinsons once wrote that the tidelands exchange was "so little understood by the citizens" that it was "difficult to get any news coverage which cited the enormous disadvantages to the public through the exchange. The public [hadn't] been made aware of exactly what it own[ed] in the upper bay."

The biggest question was if the low-lying Upper, Middle, and Shellmaker Islands were actually tidelands, and if they were, had they legally been transferred to Irvine Company hands? Could the company do what it pleased with the land, or did it hold the land "in trust" subject to public easement, meaning that land development had to benefit the State of California?

Not Economically Beneficial

On December 10, 1963, as reported in the *Daily Pilot* the next day, the Newport Beach City Council meeting got heated when Council Member James B. Stoddard said to The Irvine Company's Vice President William Mason, "Your trade isn't in the public interest. You can't argue this, and neither can I. You've heard our view right down the line."

Mason argued that the deal was in the public's best interest. Years later, in a 1970 statement published in *Irvine World News,* Mason said that it was the county that had first approached them to make a marina. He said, "When approached by the county, we cooperated believing that the land swap they suggested was in our own best interests and the best interest of those who are part of the Irvine community and the general public."

A 1965 appraisal report had said the county would have an $8,012,500 advantage if it swapped 157 acres of its tidelands for 450 acres elsewhere. In October 1968, Orange County assessor Andrew J. Hinshaw urged the Board of Supervisors to reject the deal, criticizing the trade as "legally improper" and based on "gross misstatements of probable assessed values." Later, in his December 11, 1968, written statement to the Assembly Subcommittee on Conservation and Beaches, Hinshaw said that this "alleged dollar advantage" was "highly questionable" and could not result in a net benefit to the county. "The appraiser did not properly appraise the land," Hinshaw said at the subcommittee hearing on December 12. Also, in 1971, the Ralph Nader Task Force reported, "The current county assessor estimated the value of the islands was more than 100 times the assessed valuation."

Warren Crow, an appraiser from the Newport Beach Taxpayers Association, also warned the Newport Beach City Council back in December 1963 that the valuation of the three islands in the bay was not accurate. The Right of Way department valued Middle Island at $1.1 million, but the county appraiser calculated its value at just $311, so the land would only yield $23 in taxes that year (just $3.75 of that went to the city). In 1976, Frank Robinson said during a speech to the Sierra Club, "I paid more taxes on my house than The Irvine Company paid on all those three islands."

In their December 18, 1969, letter to the Honorable George W. Milias, Chairman of the Assembly Committee on Natural Resources and Conservation in Sacramento, the Robinsons wrote that "if the deal went through, the bay would represent $150 million to $200 million dollars for The Irvine Company. The land the county would receive would only be worth $5 million and badly located with respect to flood control channels and accumulation of debris. Not only that, they said, the new proposed boundaries of the bay's shore would be filled partially at the county's expense."

The One and Only Plan

In 1963, the Orange County Board of Supervisors approved The Irvine Company's plan for a marina. County officials presented it as the best way to develop the upper bay at minimum expense, but, the Robinsons asked, how could they know it was the best plan if they had only seen one plan? And, as stated in the July 1969 press release from the grand jury, even though the county did not have money to develop the bay into a marina at the time, it did not mean they had to take the first deal that came along. When the proposal reached the State Lands Commission, for example, it was rejected, one of the reasons being the lack of any alternate plan (the commission did eventually give its approval in 1967).

In 1966, Assemblyman Jesse Unruh stated that the land exchange was not in the best interest of the public because the county supervisors had not "seriously considered possible alternatives." He said, "All the alternatives should be explored and tested before the present solution is adopted." At this time, the Robinsons, Unruh, and many other concerned citizens were actually still in favor of upper bay development, but they did not support the current plan.

A Detriment to the Environment

It took a few years for the Robinsons and many of their neighbors to fully realize the importance of the bay's ecology. In the late 1960s, people had become more environmentally conscious, and newspaper coverage of Upper Newport Bay reflected that. One 1968 *Los Angeles Times* article quoted scientists claiming that the bay represented the last publicly held estuarine-type environment and that the proposed plan would lead to water pollution. A 1969 *Daily Pilot* article quoted scientist Dr. Wheeler North as saying that his underwater studies of former bay estuaries that had been dredged now had "almost no life on the bottom." He said, "If you wonder what [the] upper bay gives us now, compare this area with areas in San Pedro or Wilmington." The papers noted how regular citizens were standing up at public hearings to speak for the migratory birds, about the importance of the bay as an outdoor biology classroom for students, and about how development could pollute Newport waters.

Animals of the Bay by the Numbers

30,000	individual birds per day in the winter
500	species of fossilized animals found
240	species of birds documented
200+	species of native plants
70	species of fish
50	percent of the animals listed as threatened or endangered in the United States that need wetlands to survive
33	species of fish that spawn in the bay
20	species of mammals
4	endangered birds: Ridgway's rail, Belding's savannah sparrow, California least tern, and least Bell's vireo
3	sensitive bird species: coastal California gnatcatcher, coastal cactus wren, and burrowing owl
1	endangered plant species: saltmarsh bird's beak

In February 1969, Frank Robinson, along with Friends of Newport Bay President Dr. Charles ("Chuck") Greening, testified at a two-day hearing in Los Angeles held by officials of the Federal Water Pollution Control Administration to gather material for a national estuarine pollution study. Chuck asked for state and federal agencies to step in to prevent "the delivery of most of this resource into private hands, and its ultimate destruction as an ecological entity." Frank echoed Chuck's plea in his statement, saying that, "in federal waters, such as Upper Newport Bay, no dredging or other altering of the ecology [should] be permitted to take place without permission from an accredited agency."

The Irvine Company, on the other hand, claimed that the pleasure harbor would actually be *good* for the environment. In addition to beaches and parks set aside for the public, the company had, by 1970, provided a "200-acre freshwater marsh and wildlife preserve for the preservation of the ecology of migratory birds and many other species of animal and plant life." As far as water quality went, "the proposed development of the harbor, since it increases the water area almost 50 percent… would, by its very nature, improve the water quality in the upper bay. Existing laws should be enforced to ensure that man will not pollute the bay… The private lands would be developed in a manner which would certainly protect the environment of the surrounding high-value homes and the lower harbor."

Newport Beach citizens gathered evidence that the proposed land exchange and development 1) could be illegal, 2) was not economically beneficial for the county, 3) was not the only option available, and 4) would be detrimental to the environment.

Of course, William Mason and The Irvine Company didn't take this information lying down. According to the March 1970 issue of *Irvine World News,* Mason suggested that "when the bay has been developed, both its public and private portions will be enjoyed by thousands of people. The owner of the private lands will be able to develop his property into a wide variety of uses; a prerogative which he has been entitled to since he purchased the land."

Just as the Robinsons and their neighbors were upset with the prospect of no longer having access to the beaches they loved, William Mason was upset that a landowner could not do with his land what he wished. The tide of public opinion was turning, and by 1969, the general public wanted to preserve Upper Newport Bay, not just provide public access.

Early Supporters

The Robinsons did not fight development of Upper Newport Bay on their own. From 1963 to 1969, before the tidelands issue went to the courts, Newport Bay had many supporters. The most enthusiastic of those supporters would form two separate organizations, Friends of Newport Bay (FONB) and Upper Newport Bay Defense Fund.

Friends of Newport Bay

Year Founded: 1967

Purpose: To increase public awareness of the unique values found in Newport Bay in order to protect and enhance the bay.

Major Players: Fern Zimmerman, Dr. Charles ("Chuck") Greening

Other Names: Over the years, Friends of Newport Bay became Newport Bay Naturalists and Friends (NBNF) when it merged in 1990 with the Upper Newport Bay Naturalists, and then in 2000 was renamed Newport Bay Conservancy.

Upper Newport Bay Defense Fund

Year Founded: 1969

Purpose: To support legal action to retain the public tidelands of Upper Newport Bay in the public domain.

Major Players: Allan Beek, Dr. Charles ("Chuck") Greening, Robert Hall, James McGaugh (Chairman), and Fern Zimmerman

Other Names: Shortly after its inception, the Defense Fund was phased out and became the Orange County Foundation for the Preservation of Public Property.

In addition, a few politicians and government officials had been on the side of the concerned citizens from the beginning, including:

Alan Sieroty, California State Assemblyman (D-Beverly Hills)

Robert Battin, Orange County Board of Supervisors

Jesse Unruh, leader of the California State Assembly and head of the State Tidelands Committee

Charles Baldwin, Special Investigator for the State Tidelands Committee

Chapter Three

Gaining Support

~⌐~

W hile their neighbors—those with interest in keeping their own access to the bay—were on the Robinsons' side from the beginning, local decision-makers, newspapers, and The Irvine Company, however, were not easy to persuade. They did not exactly welcome Frank and Fran with open arms.

Alton Allen, from the Orange County Board of Supervisors, said in the October 1, 1963 issue of the *Newport Harbor News Press*, "These people are interested in getting access to the land themselves, not in making the access a truly public one."

But Frank had never insinuated he wanted the land for himself. Frank told the *Daily Pilot* that he had gotten up to speak at the previous board of supervisors meeting to ask that, "beaches northerly of North Star Drive be opened to the public." Allen's response to Frank's clarification was, "I don't remember what he said." It was clear that early on, the board of supervisors did not take them or their public access argument seriously.

For the first few years, the Robinsons said, the papers either "painted [them] in the worst possible light" or ignored them completely. "The *Pilot* and the *[Los Angeles] Times* in the beginning gave us a very bad time," Frank said.

For example, when Frank was a major speaker at a State Lands Commission hearing in Newport Beach in 1967, Frank was "to be on the podium early so that it would make that morning's newspapers," Frances recalled. "He testified for 45 minutes, and there was not a single word in the newspaper, but they mentioned other people who had a lot less to say about other issues." One of the few politicians on their side at the time told them, "Clearly they [the newspapers] have a policy of blocking you out."

The Robinsons said that politicians and newspaper editors didn't take them seriously because they had accepted the status quo, which was that The Irvine Company was good business for Orange County. "Everybody pretty much kowtowed to The Irvine Company in the political system," Frank said, "because they were *the* political entity of the county."

The Irvine Company had offered the Robinsons somewhat of a "solution" in those early days. They could sell beach property to the Robinsons: two lots for $7,500 each. But Frank and Fran didn't have $15,000, and the whole point of their community involvement was to have public property stay public property, not become privately owned beach.

While the Robinsons and The Irvine Company couldn't reach a deal for land, it looked like the company and the local university could. On February 10, 1966, Fran wrote a note to herself, saying, "Today was the lowest point in our struggle to keep for the public the upper bay… The Irvine Company has promised to give some acreage for a park adjacent to UCI [University of California, Irvine] if the university will help get the trade passed. This …was put in the following manner: 'The Irvine Company will have some land available for a park for the university, but we will not know just how much land until we see how the upper bay trade goes.' "

The fact that the Robinsons were treated so poorly in the beginning proved to be a benefit to the bay in the long run. Lane Koluvek, a close friend of the Robinsons and future president of Friends of Newport Bay, said, "In a sense, The Irvine Company did us a great deed." They "had irked Frank so much that he wanted to fight them." Lane believed that if the development plan had been altered in the early 1960s so the public could have more access to the beaches, "Frank and Fran might have been satisfied and gone away, or the route they took would have been totally different."

Over the next few years, those who opposed them would call Frank and Fran "the dumb engineer and his bird-brained wife," "communists," and "radical kooks." One opponent accused them of trying to protect their own ocean view. Of course, they had no ocean view.

"There were some things said about us that were very unkind," Fran said. But all the insults and setbacks never made the Robinsons consider giving up. Instead, they hunkered down, dug their heels in deeper, and fought harder than before. "You have got to persevere no matter how tired you might get, no matter how angry you might get," Fran said.

Those opponents who had shrugged them off, tried to hush them up, or cracked jokes at their expense in the early 1960s would, within a few years, either come to their side or accept defeat.

———

"Where's your political clout? You've got nothing going for you unless you have political clout." In the late 1960s, Charles Baldwin, the special investigator who helped the Robinsons look deeper into the trade, asked Frank this question. They received similar advice after the board of supervisors approved the recreational harbor plan 5 to 0. An early volunteer named George Friedl, Jr. told the Robinsons, "What you have to do is change where the problem is; you've got to elect a new board of supervisors."

The idea was "to have a board that would be responsible and not always voting just for one thing, The Irvine Company," Fran said. "We thought he was nuts. How could we, two dumb bunnies, elect a new board of supervisors?"

Fran underestimated just how powerful she, Frank, and the people supporting the bay had become. The Robinsons were a big reason why a new board of supervisors was elected in 1970, which voted unanimously *against* the trade. They worked hard to gain political clout, and they—along with Friends of Newport Bay members—developed a strategy that would work well for them over the years, as outlined here.

Get Politicians to Listen

It was a waste of everyone's time when politicians wouldn't listen. "We had to learn how to talk to a city council, how to talk to commissions, how to prepare documentation," Frank said. "You have to play the game in the political arena in a language that politicians understand." When going before a council or commission, which limits the time someone can speak, they would break up the information over a few speakers. "The nice thing about breaking it up that way is that you don't bore the councilmen, you don't bore the commission. By divvying up the work into smaller digestible increments, you do a great benefit to your cause and a great service to the decision makers… They can digest and understand, and you keep from boring them to death."

Frank also said to stay focused on one issue and be friendly. He said, "If you're against everything, when you walk into a board of supervisors meeting [they'll say], 'My god, the guy's against everything. Forget it.' But if you're only against one thing, you can be friendly on the other issues."

Educate Those Politicians

Frank would do the research and create a concise, easy-to-understand presentation with solid facts and evidence. He said, "I spent an awful lot of time making sure of my information before I'd present my issue to other people." Not all education happened at meetings or in letters; politicians were always welcome for a personal tour around the bay.

In March 1965, Fran sent a letter to Jesse Unruh, the leader of the California State Assembly and head of the State Tidelands Committee. She said, "If it is possible to arrange an appointment to consult with you… concerning this matter, we should very much appreciate whatever time you might be able to give. We would also welcome the opportunity to explain the trade to you with a personal tour of the upper bay if you should be visiting this area."

A visit to the bay would make almost anyone a supporter of preservation, and this was no different for politicians. After Friends of Newport Bay members Allan Beek, Wes Marx, and Chuck Greening met with California Senator Peter H. Behr in 1972, he wrote them a thank-you letter. He said, "The background we learned on the Upper Newport Bay was most valuable. I certainly came away from our meeting more than ever convinced of the need to protect and preserve the bay."

Use Their Influence

In their letters to politicians, the Robinsons would say, "Once these tidelands are gone, they are gone forever. May we plead… that you use your influence to help defeat this trade?" Luckily, some of them did, one of those being Assemblyman Alan Sieroty. In 1970, Sieroty asked then-governor Ronald Reagan to intervene in the proposed land exchange. "If the governor is serious about his stated goal of preserving our relatively few estuaries as he said in his State-of-the-State message," Sieroty said, "then let us see some action on his part to save Upper Newport Bay, one of the last remaining estuaries on the entire West Coast."

Mobilize Supporters During Elections

The Robinsons collected signatures door-to-door. Then the Friends of Newport Bay created a mailing list. The ever-growing list of contacts meant that they could mobilize hundreds of people by writing a single letter. They could begin letter-writing campaigns to change a politician's vote, to get much-needed volunteers or donations, or to help politicians get elected.

For example, a March 5, 1972 letter from Frank and Fran asked bay supporters to elect Paul Ryckoff to the city council. They wrote, "Mr. Ryckoff, a resident of Balboa Island… not only desires to protect the quality of our environment, but he has given testimony at various hearings of the Public Utilities Commission with regard to environmental issues… If you think you would like to have Mr. Ryckoff represent you on our city council, you can help by volunteering some time, sending a contribution for his campaign expenses, telling your friends about him, and being sure to vote for him on election day." Ryckoff was elected and served on the council for eight years.

Politicians whom the Robinsons helped were appreciative. In 1971, Ronald Caspers wrote to Frank and Fran, "Your joining [my wife] Ann and me in celebrating my first year as county supervisor was an honor and most reassuring to one so new as I to the political world… I am very grateful for your support."

Fall Back to Recharge

Not only did the Robinsons need a break to prevent exhaustion, they also didn't want to pester politicians, the newspapers, and their supporters. "We would relax and go skiing and do our summer things," Fran said, although she and Frank never took too much time off from their work on the bay. "Maybe six months later, [we'd say], 'Well, it's cooled off. People have forgotten.' And we'd show up and we'd raise hell and scream and kick and all that. Write the letters, create unpleasantness for the public, and then let it cool." Following this cycle allowed them to stay energized and relevant, and stall the development in the bay. "We bought seven or eight years with very little funding just by being a nuisance," she said.

———

They had neighbors on their side. They slowly got politicians on their side. They found there was a third group that would help fight for the bay: environmentalists. From 1963 through 1968, a small group of nature-lovers offered their help, but eventually environmentalists would become the bay's most numerous support group.

The environmental movement started in the 1960s, thanks in large part to biologist Rachel Carson's book *Silent Spring,* which created a generation of environmental activists. In the book, Carson explains the harmful effects of the indiscriminate use of pesticides such as DDT. This pesticide, which causes birds to lay thinly shelled eggs that could not hatch, was the reason why Jay, playing in the bay in the 1960s, would not have seen many pelicans or ospreys. Thanks in large part to Carson's book, DDT was banned nationwide in 1972, and many threatened bird populations have since bounced back.

When the Robinsons began fighting the land exchange in 1963, environmentalism was in its infancy, and the conservative politicians, developers, and residents of Orange County could not imagine a problem developing the bay, other than those pesky residents who wanted to keep using the bay's beaches.

"We were at the absolute beginning of the environmental movement in this country," Fran said. "You can't pick up a newspaper anymore without seeing a great deal of information about some kind of an environmental disaster or battle. But in those days, there wasn't anything, not a thing."

Fern Zimmerman, who would later become Fran Robinson's good friend, had been a prominent member of the Orange County Sea & Sage chapter of the Audubon Society. An avid birder determined to save this bird haven, Fern organized and led a group of nature-lovers into creating an organization called Friends of Newport Bay (FONB).

Chuck Greening wrote about the organization's formation in a March 1998 issue of the *Fullerton Observer.* He said, "We did not want to see a prized, rare coastal wetland destroyed, as so many others in California had been." So, in 1967 "Fern organized a public meeting with panelists from the Corps of Engineers, the California Department of Fish and Game, and others. A sign-up sheet was passed around, and about a dozen of us signed up to form Friends of Newport Bay." At this meeting, Greening became the organization's first president.

Friends of Newport Bay appealed to environmentalists and became the point of contact for environmentally concerned citizens. An undated Friends brochure explained the organization to potential members. It read, "If development is carried out as agreed to by Orange County and The Irvine Company, the natural balance in the bay will be destroyed. Due to the imminent danger of this valuable, life-giving estuary being dredged out, aroused citizens joined together and formed the Friends of Newport Bay. One of the principal goals of the Friends is to increase public awareness of the unique values found in the bay. With strong public support, our local and state government will strive to protect and enhance the upper bay."

While there was some local environmentalist interest, it took an environmental disaster in early 1969 for the fight for Upper Newport Bay to really take off. It happened on Tuesday, January 28, 1969, at 10:45 a.m., 130 miles north of Newport Beach. Under a Union Oil offshore drilling rig five miles off the Santa Barbara coast, an underwater pipe blew out, cracking the sea floor around it. Over 11 days, 3 million gallons of oil gushed into the ocean. The current dispersed it across 800 square miles of the ocean and coated 35 miles of coastline. At the time it was the largest oil spill in the United States. Since then there have been two larger spills: Exxon Valdez in 1989 and Deepwater Horizon in 2010.

Volunteers from all walks of life rushed to help, despite the thick tar odor in the air and the dangers of getting oil on their own skin. Wildlife rescuers counted 3,600 dead seabirds and many poisoned seals and dolphins. The spill had devastated the kelp forests, killed an unknown number of fish and invertebrates, and displaced endangered birds that lived and fed in the area. It took years for the ecosystem to recover.

President Richard Nixon, who came to view the damage personally, said, "The Santa Barbara incident has frankly touched the conscience of the American people." It was true. The Santa Barbara oil spill sparked the modern environmental movement and resulted in the first Earth Day in 1970, the Environmental Protection Agency, and the California Coastal Commission. These agencies, "if they had been in existence when we first started this protest," said Frank, "would never have approved the upper bay trade."

The devastating oil spill also resulted in a great deal of interest in Upper Newport Bay. "The Santa Barbara oil spill actually worked to our advantage," Frank said, "It gave national recognition to a serious coastal problem."

In late 1968, Friends of Newport Bay held its first "Friends Tour." Naturalists guided visitors on a tour between outdoor "classrooms" set up along Back Bay Drive. In retrospect, that first tour was just a dress rehearsal for the February 15, 1969, tour, held one week after the oil in Santa Barbara stopped gushing. While cleanup was still underway in Santa Barbara, 1,000 people showed up at Vista Point in Newport Beach early that Saturday morning, ready to learn more about Upper Newport Bay.

Part Two | The Battle in Full-Swing

Chapter Four

FIGHTING ON TWO FRONTS

In January and February 1969, 40 inches of rain fell on Southern California, making 1969 the wettest year on record up to that point. The Santa Ana River overflowed, mudslides and water destroyed homes and businesses in more than a dozen cities, and the Silverado Canyon Mudslide took five lives and injured 17.

Upper Newport Bay was severely impacted, as Jack E. Hemphill of the U.S. Fish and Wildlife Service described in a letter to the Los Angeles District Corps of Engineers. "Land use practices are having a direct and indirect impact on Upper Newport Bay as a self-renewing resource," Hemphill said. "Recent large-scale developments on the bluffs adjacent to the upper bay have involved massive reshaping of the bluffs and slopes and the gross removal of native vegetative cover. Following this denuding, the rains of the winter of 1968-1969 took their toll; excessive corrosion of the bluffs and upland areas resulted in massive amounts of mud, silt, and other debris being dumped into Upper Newport Bay, covering the salt marshes and tide flats and wrecking the salt works. Feeding and resting areas utilized by numerous species of migratory birds, including waterfowl, marsh birds, and shorebirds, were degraded or destroyed. Bottom organisms within the bay were covered by a layer of silt."

It was likely raining in Newport Beach the day each *Sunset Magazine* subscriber received the February 1969 issue, which promoted the Upper Newport Bay Friends Tour. The article suggested bringing binoculars to see the winter birds, mentioned flowers that might be in bloom, and described places to picnic. This short article, which brought hundreds of people to the bay, read, in part:

> The future of Upper Newport Bay is the subject of a great deal of public attention in Orange County: this presently wild salt marsh may become a development site like Newport Harbor. The charms of the 'Back Bay' are not obvious to the casual onlooker, but for an interpretation of its significance you can join a guided tour on Saturday, February 15. The tour begins at 9 a.m. A botanist, a marine ecologist, bird observers, and archeology and nature guides will lecture at six or more locations on the various aspects of the upper bay's distinctive environment. You can walk the 2-mile route or drive the mostly dirt road along the edge of the bay and stop at the stations for the lectures.

Because the oil spill in Santa Barbara stopped gushing just one week before the Saturday of the scheduled tour, and because several other outlets picked up on the new Friends Tours, there was a lot of interest. But in the early morning of Saturday, February 15, torrential rains caused many of the tour guides to think no one would show up and the tour would be canceled.

Chuck Greening, first president of Friends of Newport Bay, was scheduled to man the "Bird Stop" on the tour that morning. He told the *Los Angeles Times* in 1990 that after the *Sunset* article, which had his phone number printed in it, people started calling at 5 a.m. to ask if the rain affected that day's tour. Even though the storms had ruptured the main dike a half-mile from where the tour was to begin and mud was sliding down the bluffs and into the bay, the tour was on. Even in the pouring rain, people came from more than 100 miles away.

"Over 1,000 people turned out in that pouring rain," Chuck said. "None of us ever dreamed that someone would wake up in Barstow at four in the morning and climb in their car and drive to the bay for the tour. I don't think any of us dreamed there were people that far away who were interested."

Just like Chuck, Frank Robinson began getting calls from all over Southern California in the early morning hours. "Is the walk still on?" they asked. "'Of course,' I said, 'of course it is.' Looking out my [window], I couldn't see across the yard, it was raining so hard!"

Upper Newport Bay by the Numbers

2	how many times a day the tides sweep into and out of the bay, exchanging lower bay water with the upper bay
3	average water depth in feet (outside the main dredged channel, which is 14 feet deep)
3.5	length of the bay in miles (it is about a half a mile wide)
5	percent of California's coastal wetlands that still exist and remain intact
6	different habitats: open water, mudflat, saltmarsh, freshwater marsh, riparian, and upland
10	percent of California's wetlands that have not been developed
20	deepest depth in feet at high tide
85	percent of freshwater that enters the bay comes from one source (San Diego Creek)
90	percent of the natural resource value of the bay that would have been destroyed had development gone forward
100	height of the tallest cliff in feet
154	square miles of Newport Bay's current watershed (it was just 60 square miles before urbanization)
1,000	approximate acres of open space
1975	year the Ecological Reserve was dedicated
7,000-9,000	number of years ago that native people established villages in the area
381,000	acres of estuary and other coastal wetlands in California before 1900
500,000+	visitors to the bay each year

Biologist Lance Gilbertson, who would later discover two new land snail species along the U.S.-Mexico border, volunteered at the "Mud Stop" that Saturday in 1969. "The day of that tour was really something," he said. "I thought for sure the tour would be canceled… How many people would show up in rain like this in Southern California? Well, more than 1,000 people showed up that morning. There were buses from Barstow and locals and people from Los Angeles—they just came from all over the place. It was incredible. People didn't care about the rain. They were so taken with this new movement that they came no matter what.

"And so we gave the tours," Lance said, "getting soaked out there but still having fun. Frank Robinson was the first on the tour stop, and he [talked] about the politics of what [had] been going on the last couple of years, and then people would go station to station." There were so many people that the volunteers did their talks multiple times.

In a two-part *Orange County Illustrated* article in the early 1970s titled "Endangered Species—Endangered Environment on Tour in Upper Newport Bay," writer Greg Smith described a later Friends Tour, when the sun was shining. "From the top of the hill where the tour begins [the intersection of Back Bay Drive and East Bluff], a vast panorama of the bay unfolds. Across are the green hills below Palisades Road: to the east a glimpse of the San Joaquin Marsh and the channel cut by San Diego Creek into the upper bay. Down the hill the road turns from pavement to dirt, and although a sign warns that passage may be impossible in the winter, the land is dry most of the time. To the right of the road are thickets of tough, wiry brush, and occasional blossoms of wild tobacco. To the left, the hill steepens into a sheer cliff, and at the base of it we amazingly find sewer installations—a little premature work by The Irvine Company in anticipation of a proposed land exchange with the county…

"Fine black soil banks the borders and uplands which used to be lapped by small boat wakes at every high tide. Much of the soil washed into the bay following the heavy winter flooding of 1968-1969, but this year's soil runoff from new housing developments on the adjacent bluff has compounded the problem. Nutrients (such as fertilizer) added to the water have produced a bumper crop of algae—a growth more destructive than beneficial when it begins to choke off other life forms."

Frances Robinson, easily recognized in her often-worn, extra-large straw hat, began her talk about development in the bay with tiny Anna's hummingbirds feeding on the tubular flowers behind her. At the second stop, Hal Fitzwater from Golden West College discussed the geological formation of the bay. Another 200 feet down the road and past a large flock of American coots, John Wilkerson began his explanation of the bay's plant life. Ray Williams, biology instructor at Rio Hondo College in Whittier, presented fish preserved in jars, and finishing the tour was Chuck Greening, who set up telescopes for the group, and he discussed the birds.

These Friends Tours were set up to educate the public about Upper Newport Bay and its importance. Once the public saw the bay and understood it, they would be more likely to fight for it and fight against the Orange County-Irvine Company land swap. Linda Koluvek, Treasurer of the Friends, worked a table where she sold T-shirts, mugs, and other souvenirs, and took donations. She also signed people up for memberships for just $1 and put the new member's address on the Friends' mailing list. Chuck Greening said that at each monthly Friends Tour, "some fraction of these 'tourists' became Friends members. When called upon, these folks could and did generate thousands of supporting letters at crucial times in the political process affecting the bay."

After taking a Friends Tour, no one could deny the beauty, uniqueness, and importance of Upper Newport Bay. "It may just look like mud," *Orange County Illustrated* writer Greg Smith said, "but if you think it is, look again. It's really the key to the ocean, and the ocean looks frailer every day."

———

In the early days, the Robinsons worked with newspapers to educate people about the public access issue of the land trade. Now the Friends of Newport Bay used the papers to invite people to visit the bay, the thought being that once people saw the bay in person, they would want to save it for the public as an ecological reserve. Friends Tours were advertised in the *Pilot*, the *Orange County Register,* and other small papers.

Linda Koluvek, Friends treasurer, said, "Fran wrote a regular newsletter [and] would always put in there the next tour dates that were held on the second Saturday of the month, October through March." Linda, after meeting bicyclists who stopped by her table asking for information but unable to carry anything in their small pockets, came up with the idea of a foldable wallet card with information, including the tour dates. Friends Tours were even mentioned by Phil Hughes on the local news, and there was always word of mouth.

In the 1970s, a lot of supporters and volunteers came from Fullerton College when it offered a mini-course titled "Upper Newport Bay: An Ecosystem in an Urban Environment" with Chuck Schneebeck as professor. His students would come to the bay for class. The bay obviously had an effect on Chuck's students, as it did for most people who visited the bay. "About one third of them stuck around, and they became a part of our organization," said Friends President Lane Koluvek. "That's how we got a lot of people to help with the tours" up until about 1985, when the mini-course was no longer offered at the college.

No matter how the Friends got the word out, the public connection to the bay was no doubt vital for its salvation. "Don't sell the public relations aspect of any of these projects short," said Frank Robinson. It's "terribly important to the people to identify with what you're trying to do."

Two Organizations, One Objective

Legal counsel advised Frank and Frances to keep the political and educational sides of the campaign separate. This way the Robinsons could steer clear of the "kooky birdwatching hippie" image, which was not held in high esteem at the time. They would be taken more seriously by important decision-makers this way.

Frank and Fran were officially associated with the Orange County Foundation for the Preservation of Public Property. They were active in the Friends of Newport Bay, attending just about every meeting and Friends Tour, but the Robinsons weren't officially a part of the Friends. They didn't even sign membership papers until 1978, after the battle was over.

Lane Koluvek, president of the Friends from 1988-2000, said that the Foundation (previously the Upper Newport Bay Defense Fund) "didn't want to be associated with the Friends in the eyes of the public or the courts. Even though they were involved, and clearly they were, they were saying that the organization was separate. You could never say that organization was the arm of the other one."

Frank said, "To a large degree, they [the Friends] operated fairly independently of us for a long time, which was fine because we all had the same objective, to preserve the bay."

"The battle to save the bay was fought on two fronts," wrote Leslie Earnest in the March 4, 1990, issue of the *Los Angeles Times*. "While nature lovers plugged into the growing environmentalist movement to keep the spotlight on the 'Back Bay,' others whittled away at the legal agreements between the county and The Irvine Company. It was on the legal front that the major battle was won."

For years there was talk that the highly contested land exchange would need to be settled in the courts. It looked like this would finally happen in 1969 when the Orange County auditor, V.A. Heim, received a bill from The Irvine Company. The company believed that the county would pay for certain engineering costs incurred while dredging the bay, but Heim refused to pay the bill. Not only that, title companies wanted a court decision stating that The Irvine Company owned the land and could legally build on it before allowing the property to be insured.

Because the County of Orange, The Irvine Company, and the Orange County Harbor District all wanted the trade and subsequent development, they joined to set up a "friendly lawsuit" to finalize this business. In a friendly suit, parties agree to enter a lawsuit to resolve a legal question or obtain a legal opinion on an issue. There is no plaintiff, no defendant, and no jury.

With the friendly suit, the county, The Irvine Company, and the harbor district wanted to obtain two things: 1) a writ of mandate to compel Heim to issue payment of the county's agreed share of costs and 2) declarations that several agreements were valid and in compliance with the enabling legislation and the California Constitution.

Everything the Robinsons had been fighting for was at stake. If the judge found the land trade to comply with the constitution, the pleasure marina could be developed and the bay would be lost forever. But if the judge found the trade to be unconstitutional, the bay would be free from development by The Irvine Company… at least for the time being.

A Sierra Club member and lawyer named Ralph Perry from the Los Angeles law firm Grossman, Smaltz, Graven & Perry, suggested that the Robinsons enter into the lawsuit as intervenors so they could present their evidence and legal opinions as well.

Intervenors have a lot of power in a friendly lawsuit. With a court action, for example, as a member of the public, you can attend, and if the court gives permission, you can put in a few words. "You can't present evidence, factual data, nothing like that," said Frank. "The judge has extreme control." But as intervenors, the Robinsons would be on equal footing with The Irvine Company, able to present evidence and cross-examine. Luckily the Orange County Foundation for the Preservation of Public Property could pay Ralph Perry, who, as the Robinsons understood, would charge a minimum—just $5,000.

Ralph Perry's plan was to have Frank and Fran Robinson and two other couples, Wes and Judy Marxes, and Hal and Joan Coverdale, intervene in the case as three families, which they thought would be good publicity. They submitted paperwork to intervene in April 1969.

They figured they'd be rejected, but to everyone's surprise, they were accepted as intervenors. "We thought we did it on our own merit, and boy, were we proud," said Frank. "But we didn't have a damn thing to do with the decision." It was Charlie O'Brian, Assistant Attorney General, who told the lawyers representing the State to let the Robinsons, Marxes, and Coverdales in. The lawsuit needed to be airtight, otherwise the friendly suit wouldn't stand upon appeal.

On April 19, 1969, the Robinsons, Marxes, and Coverdales were officially a part of case number M-1105, County of Orange and The Irvine Company v. V. A. Heim, the State of California, and Frank and Frances Robinson, Harold and Joan Coverdale, and Wesley and Judith Marx, as residents and taxpayers of the County of Orange.

But now there was a problem. The estimate of $5,000 in legal fees did not take into consideration the intervenors being accepted right away. So, at the last minute, Perry said he needed $75,000 for discovery, and neither the Orange County Foundation for the Preservation of Public Property nor the intervenors had that kind of money in the bank.

Frank and Frances Robinson on the bluffs overlooking Newport Bay.
Photo by Jay Robinson.

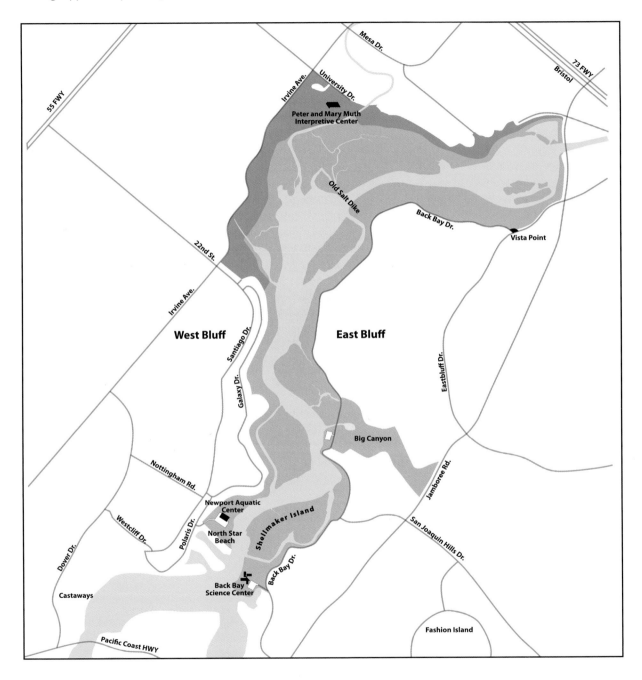

Left: *A map of Upper Newport Bay showing what today's visitors can visit in the park. Note that the Robinson's North Star Beach is now the location of the Newport Aquatic Center, where paddlers can launch their kayaks and other watercraft. Image by Jim Cokas.*

Upper Right: *The salt works operation in the 1960s. In 1934, dikes and evaporating ponds were built in the upper reaches of the bay to harvest 5,000 tons of salt per year. Photo courtesy Orange County Archives.*

Lower Right: *A quiet Upper Newport Bay pictured in 1919 before the Orange County population boom, and before salt and shells were harvested from the bay for commercial purposes. Photo courtesy Orange County Archives.*

Visitors launching their boats on an Upper Newport Bay beach. Waterskiing was a popular sport here in the 1960s, even with the Robinsons.
Photographer unknown.

Newport Dredging Company on Shellmaker Island. From 1939 to the late 1980s, up to 1,200 tons of ancient shell deposits each month were dredged and ground into a calcium supplement for chicken feed. Photographer unknown.

A young Frances Robinson in the early days of the fight to save the bay. From Fran Robinson's photo album, donated to the UCI Archives.

An older Frank Robinson at one of the many Friends of Newport Bay parties (undated).
From Fran Robinson's photo album, donated to the UCI Archives.

Undated photo of Fern Zimmerman, an early member of the Sea & Sage Audubon Society, member of the League of Women Voters, and co-founder of Friends of Newport Bay. Photo courtesy Sea & Sage Audubon Society.

Chuck Greening receiving an award from Friends of Newport Bay on May 9, 1991, before he and his wife, A.J., moved to New Mexico. Chuck was integral in saving the bay, co-founding the Friends of Newport Bay in 1967 and even testifying at the friendly lawsuit in 1970. Also in the picture is Lane Koluvek.
From Fran Robinson's photo album, donated to the UCI Archives.

ABOVE: *View of Upper Newport Bay from Westcliff, the Robinsons' neighborhood, in June 1967. Boats could often be seen on the water pulling water-skiers behind them.*
Photo by John W. Johnson.

RIGHT: *One of the many "Private Property" signs that The Irvine Company posted around Upper Newport Bay.*
Photo by Bill Halladay.

RIGHT TO PASS BY PERMISSION AND SUBJECT TO CONTROL OF THE IRVINE COMPANY
SECTION 1008 CIVIL CODE

Built in 1969, The Irvine Company headquarters at 500 and 550 Newport Center Drive (the two identical buildings in the center of the complex) are visible in this 1975 photo across the bay. The Fashion Island shopping complex, which opened in 1967, is right next door.
Photo by Charles O'Rear of the Environmental Protection Agency, courtesy the U.S. National Archives.

Marine biology teacher Ray Williams working the "Mud Stop" during a 1972 Friends Tour. Still from the film The Back Bay, by Environmental Ethic Films, copyright 1972 Gary Rogers.

Ray brought specimens in jars to each tour and showed them to visitors out of the back of his car (shown here). His license plate read "BAKBAY." Photographer unknown.

Orange County auditor V.A. "Vic" Heim, shown here at his desk in 1981, refused to reimburse The Irvine Company for certain engineering costs on their early work in the bay. His refusal to pay was one of the reasons for the friendly lawsuit. Photo courtesy Orange County Archives.

29. Phillip S. Berry 1969-1971

President of the Sierra Club (1969-1971 and 1991-1992) and trial attorney from Oakland, Phil Berry represented the Robinsons and other intervenors in the 1970 lawsuit and appeal. Photo courtesy of the Sierra Club Library.

Trial lawyer Phil Berry protesting Standard Oil after the 1969 Santa Barbara Oil Spill. Photo courtesy of the Sierra Club Library.

Kenneth A. Sampson, Director of Harbors, Beaches and Parks, was called to testify at the friendly lawsuit for seven days. He is pictured here giving items to Miss Dana Point, Nancy Buenger, to be placed in a time capsule at a ceremony to mark the beginning of construction at Dana Point Harbor in 1966.
Photo courtesy Orange County Archives.

Orange County Supervisor Ronald Caspers was a vocal supporter of the bay and open space throughout the county. He is pictured at Starr Viejo Regional Park circa 1973, which was renamed Ronald W. Caspers Wilderness Park to honor him after his death.
Photo courtesy Orange County Archives.

A gathering of friends on North Star Beach in the summer of 1970, while the friendly trial took place. Standing at left is Allan Beek, who testified at the trial and helped fight for the bay in numerous ways for decades. Intervenor Joan Coverdale sits beside him (in head scarf), and her husband Harold Coverdale is pictured third from right. Rodger Hedgecock, law student who assisted the Robinsons' lawyer Phil Berry, sits with his back to the camera, and the grown-up Jay Robinson—on summer break from attending law school at the University of California, Los Angeles—sits at far right.
From Fran Robinson's photo album, donated to the UCI Archives.

LEFT: *As the mascot of Upper Newport Bay, the great blue heron's silhouette has been depicted on T-shirts, car decals, and other fundraising items for decades. It even appears on the current Newport Bay Conservancy logo. In addition to the great blue heron, more than 200 species of birds visit Upper Newport Bay, including four endangered species and three critical species.*
Photo by Holly Fuhrer.

BELOW: *Although the bay was not developed into a marina like the lower bay, the land around the park has since been built up. Note the massive Tustin Hangars in the top right of this 1975 photo.*
Photo by Charles O'Rear of the Environmental Protection Agency, courtesy the U.S. National Archives.

Left to right: Frank Robinson, Newport Beach Mayor Don Strauss, and former president of The Irvine Company Ray Watson on July 25, 1989, at the dedication of Upper Newport Bay Regional Park. The Irvine Company donated 114 acres of land to the county to expand the park.
From Fran Robinson's photo album, donated to the UCI Archives. Copyright 1989 Valerie Reed.

Frances Robinson is shown at the dedication ceremony.
From Fran Robinson's photo album, donated to the UCI Archives. Copyright 1989 Valerie Reed.

Buck Johns (right) was instrumental in helping Frank Robinson block the extension of the nearby University Drive into a four-to-six-lane highway in the late 1980s. He is pictured with John Scholl from the California Department of Fish and Game.
From Fran Robinson's photo album, donated to the UCI Archives.

Frank Robinson, Linda Koluvek, Lane Koluvek, and Frances Robinson celebrating Earth Day at the University of California, Irvine, in 1990. The Koluveks and Robinsons were close friends for many years. Lane was the president of Friends of Newport Bay for 12 years, and Linda the treasurer. From Fran Robinson's photo album, donated to the UCI Archives.

In the 1990s, Frank and Fran continued to greet guests to the bay on Friends Tours. From left to right are Fran in her signature straw hat, Frank, and volunteers Lois and Ed Sockerson.
From Fran Robinson's photo album, donated to the UCI Archives.

While Fran worked the check-in table, Frank told the bay's story at the "History Stop."
From Fran Robinson's photo album, donated to the UCI Archives.

The undeveloped land in this photo shows the future site of the Peter and Mary Muth Interpretive Center. The center, which opened 25 years after this photo was taken, would be on the top left of this image. Next to the current center is the Delhi Channel (on left) and the San Diego Creek (on right), where fresh water enters the bay. The salt dike is visible here, six years after the salt works operation was closed after major flooding washed away the 1969 harvest. Saddleback Mountain can be seen in the distance.
Photo by Charles O'Rear of the Environmental Protection Agency, courtesy the U.S. National Archives.

Jack Keating speaks at the Peter and Mary Muth Interpretive Center's grand opening in 2000. Jack was President of Upper Newport Bay Naturalists and of Newport Bay Naturalists and Friends for 10 years, and a major fundraiser for the interpretive center. A generous grant from the Keating family made this book possible. Photographer unknown.

Mary and Peter Muth at the center named for them. Owners of Orco Block, Inc. in Stanton, the Muths generously donated $1 million to the Orange County parks department.
From Fran Robinson's photo album, donated to the UCI Archives.

Frank, Frances, and friends in front of their "Saving Upper Newport Bay" exhibit in the Muth Center. Sitting, left to right: Ed and Lois Sockerson, Frank and Frances Robinson. Standing, left to right: Beverly Ann Krassner-Bulas, Phil Hughes, a long-time Friends Tour volunteer, Roger Reinke, Lance Gilbertson, Lorna Houck, Ray Williams, and Dick Kust. Lance Gilbertson and Ray Williams were Friends Tour volunteers in the early years. From Fran Robinson's photo album, donated to the UCI Archives.

A 2018 satellite image of Upper Newport Bay and the built-up surrounding area.
Credit: Image © 2018 Google LLC. All rights reserved.

View of the northeast side of Upper Newport Bay as it is today. Taken near the Jamboree Road bridge and the San Diego Creek, this photo shows the manmade Tern Island, which provides a breeding area for the endangered California least tern.
Credit: Courtesy OC Helicopters.

Today Upper Newport Bay has 1,000 acres of open space, critical for migrating birds and other wildlife that calls the bay home. It is a popular destination for those who enjoy birdwatching, jogging, hiking, bicycling, and kayaking. The Muth Center can be seen tucked into the bluffs on the left.
Photo copyright Pedro Gutierrez, Shutterstock.

The Peter and Mary Muth Interpretive Center, Frances Robinson's dream for the bay for decades. She attended the grand opening in 2000 less than a year before her passing in 2001. Today visitors learn about life in and around the estuary and why Upper Newport Bay is such an important place.
Photo by Bill Halladay.

Vista Point, at the corner of Back Bay Drive and Eastbluff Drive, has been the starting point for the Friends Tours since 1968. A memorial for the Robinsons stands here today.
Credit: Photo by Bill Halladay.

Chapter Five

The Trial

❧

Frank and Frances Robinson were upset that Ralph Perry's fee skyrocketed at the last minute. Everyone was scrambling, figuring out how they would come up with the money. But they just couldn't do it.

Allan Beek, trustee of the Orange County Foundation for the Preservation of Public Property, said, "The expensive part was the lawsuit. If we had to pay regular legal fees for that, we just couldn't have done it." His wife, Jean, said, "I thought I was going to have to mortgage my house. A bad feeling… We were all wondering where we were going to get the money."

On the Friday one week before the trial, their lawyer Ralph Perry said, "I'd better withdraw you from the trial." The six intervenors had actually signed withdrawal papers, but Frances Robinson convinced them not to submit the papers.

She said, "We're about due for a miracle. Let's tell the lawyer not to withdraw *us* from the suit. He should withdraw *himself* from the suit."

He did. In his letter to the Sierra Club in San Francisco, Ralph Perry said he withdrew because they couldn't work out the finances.

Word got out to the newspapers; reporters called and asked Frank what would happen. "Oh, we've got something planned," he told them. In reality, Frank said, "I didn't know what the hell to do!"

Just as Fran foresaw, they did have a miracle. A woman from the Sierra Club named Beatrice Laws called and put them in touch with the President of the Sierra Club, Phil Berry, who was a trial attorney from Berry, Davis & McInerney from Oakland, California. He would be down in Los Angeles at a small conference at UCLA that Saturday. Laws suggested that Berry and the Robinsons meet and discuss the case.

Their meeting went well. Frank recalled that while reviewing their documents, Berry said, "You didn't need $75,000 for discovery. You've got it here!" Berry reduced his fee by 50 percent and even threw in a free law student. Berry's assistant on this case was a second-year law student named Roger Hedgecock.

They got their miracle of a lawyer they could afford, but there was still one little problem. Trial would begin in just two days.

———

On that first day in court in June 1970, Frank said later in a speech to the Sierra Club, "Irvine walks into the court with a barrel of evidence, testimony, all kinds of goodies. And in comes Phil, who's had about a day to study the case… Irvine knows we're in the hole $3,000, we haven't prepared a case, we haven't interviewed anybody, we've done nothing."

Berry asked the judge for a three-week delay. He needed time to study the information and also because his mother-in-law was dying of cancer. Her doctor had given her a week or two to live, maybe three. Berry also had three young children and lived 400 miles away in Oakland.

The judge said Berry could have five days. "We went into the trial with no preparation," Frank said. Frank would later call Claude A. Owens "a hostile judge and unfair." It did not look like it would go well for the intervenors.

On Monday, June 29, the first day of the trial, bay supporters filled the courtroom—about 50 or 60 people. The Irvine Company was represented by Gibson, Dunn & Crutcher. Attorneys for Orange County were Adrian Kuyper and Robert F. Nuttman. For the Orange County Harbor District was Rimel, Harvey & Logan and Duffern H. Helsing. Berry had reviewed Ralph Perry's work and found no reason to change his prepared arguments. At 9:50 a.m., Judge Owens said, "All right, gentlemen. The moving party may proceed." Mr. Nuttman replied, "Very well. We wish to call Mr. Kenneth Sampson, your Honor, as the first witness for the petitioners."

In the intervenors' brief, which the first lawyer Ralph Perry submitted before the trial, they laid out the intervenors' main arguments. In court, Berry argued that the trade proposal did not meet the requirements of Chapter 2044 (that County tidelands and submerged lands may be improved if not useful for navigation, commerce, and fisheries), and neither the trade proposal nor Chapter 2044 met the constitutional standards applicable to the tidelands trust. Berry would try to convince Judge Owens of the following:

1. That it could not clearly be established that the land was not useful for navigation, commerce, and fishing;
2. That realignment and relocation of the public waterways as proposed would diminish the greater public use;
3. That the development would convert public waterways into a captive waterway primarily for the use of private residential boat owners;
4. That it would create commercial areas completely privately controlled, leading to private domination of the bay.

"Obviously, this is an extraordinary case," Berry said to Judge Owens later in the trial. "This is a so-called friendly suit in which, before the intervenors became involved, it was a public trust that would be violated by the friendly action of County administrators, whose action, I think, can be shown by evidence… to have been totally irrelevant and incompetent." Other than his clients, Berry said, there was no one in the lawsuit trying to represent the public interest.

Throughout the six-week trial—which went from Monday, June 29 to Tuesday, August 18, 1970, with some days off in between—Berry would take a plane from Oakland in the morning, and the Robinsons would pick him up at the airport at 8:30. They'd brief him on the way to court, which started at 9 a.m. at the new courthouse on Civic Center Drive in Santa Ana. While court was in session, Frances would dash out to get information, and Berry's assistant, Roger Hedgecock, would go to the library for research. Berry also had Frances watch the other side's facial expressions in court and report their reactions back to him.

The trial covered public access and prescriptive rights; what information was shown to the Board of Supervisors; the economic impact the land exchange would have on Orange County; the impact the exchange would have on the natural resources of the bay; the need for comprehensive planning; who was thought to have owned what land; and if the statement that the land was not useful for navigation, commerce, and fishing, was even true.

On the second day and last day of the trial there were trips around the bay, one by car and one by boat. The star witness was Kenneth A. Sampson, Director of Harbors, Beaches and Parks, who testified for the first seven days. Other witnesses included:

- Andrew Hinshaw, Orange County Assessor
- Felix Smith, wildlife biologist with the Department of the Interior
- James P. Tryner, Department of Parks and Recreation California
- Virgil J. Butler, attorney with the State Lands Commission
- Allan Beek, who had tract map and survey experience while working with his father in real estate development
- Charles Greening, current president of Friends of Newport Bay
- Wesley Marx, writer of *Frail Ocean* and the only intervenor to testify
- Dr. Wheeler James North, kelp forester and Caltech scientist

While Berry and the intervenors were winging it—Berry sometimes mixing up the terms "patent lands" and "tidelands" and referencing the wrong maps during examination, which his own witnesses would correct him on—The Irvine Company never had less than three or four well-prepared attorneys in court. Surprisingly, The Irvine Company never challenged the intervenors on their figures and facts.

The Irvine Company's facts and figures did come in to question, however. To some it seemed the company did not always present the whole truth. Back in December 1963, Newport Beach City Council Member Donald Elder criticized a map from The Irvine Company, saying it looked like "drawings my young son could do." Again, here in court, bad maps came back to haunt The Irvine Company. Berry argued that a map, on which the company based many of its exhibits, was misleading because it didn't show Back Bay Road, an important public access point. Another map, which was shown to the Board of Supervisors and the State Lands Commission, pictured North Star Beach as an unfilled waterway, which was not the case.

The intervenors' lawyer Phil Berry said The Irvine Company must have known about these inaccuracies. "They were intimately involved in the proposed trade," he said during the trial. "They were intimately involved in all of the development of the proposal which is now here in court. They had ample opportunity to correct these misconceptions laid before the public… and most specifically, Mr. Mason [President of The Irvine Company] himself had such an opportunity."

According to court transcripts, after one of The Irvine Company lawyers tried to convince the judge that it wasn't important and that it was not William Mason's responsibility to correct these things, Berry lost his temper. He said to Judge Owens, "Now, Your Honor, frankly, I find it more than just a little annoying to have the attorney for Irvine come in here and try to swan song us with these lullabies about how it didn't make any difference… When you add all these things together, there has been a gross misrepresentation before the State Lands Commission, and that representation, that false representation, is traceable to Irvine… I think it's plain on the face of this record that the State Lands Commission was duped."

In the afternoons, Judge Owens allowed trial to end at 4 instead of 5 p.m. so Berry could catch his 4:30 flight back to Oakland. On the first day of trial, Judge Owens said, "It's a few minutes after noon now. When we were last together there was some request that we might recess early in the afternoon to accommodate Mr. Berry… Does 4 o'clock enable you to make your connection at the airport?" Berry replied, "I think so." Luckily, he was able to make his flight home.

On the way to the airport, Frank said, "he'd outline what we'd do [for our next day in court], we'd go back [home], prepare the documents, the data, the maps, the charts, Roger [Berry's assistant] would go to the library, we'd study and prepare the briefing for Phil, and he'd be back in the morning." Roger stayed at the Robinsons' house. In the evenings, they grilled (even holding one Back Bay Bash fundraiser) and hung out at the North Star Beach they were fighting for. Frances wrote in her photo album next to a snapshot of people on North Star Beach in the summer of 1970, "These people were ardent opponents of the proposed tidelands exchange and ardent supporters of the intervenors." Pictured were the Beeks, the Coverdales, Roger Hedgecock, the Robinsons' son, Jay, and others.

Three weeks into the trial, Phil Berry's mother-in-law died. He asked the judge to have Monday off for the funeral, but Owens denied the request.

The trial lasted six weeks, with 20 witnesses, more than 100 exhibits, and two inspections of the bay itself, before the court rendered its opinion. Berry charged for 29 days at trial at $250 per diem, equaling $7,250, much less than their previous lawyer's bill of $75,000 just for discovery.

The Robinsons, the other intervenors, other supporters, and Phil Berry had sacrificed a lot for this case. Yet, they lost. On December 18, 1970, Orange County Superior Court Judge Claude A. Owens ruled the trade constitutional.

During trial, Phil Berry had said to Judge Owens, "I don't see how anyone can honestly come to any other conclusion knowing what the true facts are. It's not just a question of interpretation. We are dealing with millions of dollars of real estate which Irvine would dearly love to have, and so would the people—[just] not to use for the same purposes."

"We knew we were going to lose," Frank said, but it wasn't Phil Berry's fault. He "did a good job," Frank said in a 1972 letter to Cole Wilbur of the Sierra Club Foundation. "I think Phil would have won with just about any judge other than Owens… The worst Christmas present we ever received was Judge Owens' opinion in December 1970 in favor of The Irvine Company."

———

Not only did supporters Upper Newport Bay lose the lawsuit, some also lost friendships. Two distinct sides had formed, and it was hard to stay friends throughout the contentious battle if you were on different sides. One bay supporter who lost a friend was Allan Beek, trustee of the Orange County Foundation for the Preservation of Public Property. Allan, who said he had "a foot in each camp," lost his friendship with none other than The Irvine Company's President William R. Mason.

Allan had become "a bit torn" about the role his dad, Joseph A. Beek, had to play in developing the lower bay. "He came down here in 1913 to work his way through college selling lots on Balboa Island," Allan said in an interview for this book. "He dredged one half to make the Balboa yacht basin and put the sand over on the other side to make the subdivision that's now called Beacon Bay." He could understand his dad's desire to develop the lower bay, but he could also understand the Robinsons' desire for public access to the upper bay.

William R. Mason joined The Irvine Company in 1959 as Administrative Engineer. "When he became President, I of course congratulated him," Allan said. "My first wife and I were good friends with Bill Mason and his wife… But then the upper bay began to interfere with us."

According to *Irvine Ranch: A Time for People,* written by Martin A. Brower, Director of Public Relations for The Irvine Company from 1973 to 1985, "Bill Mason was deeply hurt" by the legal battle and "was stunned by the negative reaction of the politicians and the news media." From Mason's perspective, he couldn't understand why everyone, even his friends, had turned on him.

For Upper Newport Bay supporters in 1970, things indeed looked bleak. But they were not about to give up.

Chapter Six

The Appeal

~⌒~

Although the trade was ruled constitutional, the fight was not over. The intervenors filed an objection to Owens' conclusion in January 1971 and went to the Court of Appeal in April. Soon after the ruling, there were three court actions regarding the bay. The intervenors had appealed, The Irvine Company filed a suit to force the county to go through with the trade, and the county also filed a suit regarding public access rights on The Irvine Company's land in and around Upper Newport Bay. As the appellate court said several years later, "This proceeding was commenced in the lower court as a 'friendly suit.' It has developed into a truly adversary litigation of substantial proportions."

Between 1970 and 1973—after Owens' ruling but before the appellate court ruling—several major events occurred that worked in the Robinsons' favor:

1. An important California Supreme Court decision
2. An independent report analyzing the bay trade
3. A new Orange County Board of Supervisors vote
4. A proposition that would protect California's coastline was on the ballot
5. The Irvine Company got a new president

The Supreme Court on State Trust Lands

In 1971 the California Supreme Court ruled on a similar case, Whitney v. Marks. For the purpose of development, Larry H. Marks began filling in his patented tidelands in Marin County, which the State granted to his predecessor in 1874. The Supreme Court restated and clarified the law concerning the protection of lands subject to the public trust; they explicitly expanded the public trust notion to include preserving land in its natural state. This legal precedent meant Upper Newport Bay could be saved as an ecological reserve, exactly what the Robinsons and the Friends of Newport Bay wanted.

The Ralph Nader Task Force Report

In 1971 the Ralph Nader Task Force published an independent report titled "Power and Land in California." The report described Judge Claude Owens' ruling as "tortured reasoning to misinterpret the law." It also stated that during the task force's interview with him, The Irvine Company President William Mason "referred to the Upper Bay as a 'a great big mudhole' and denigrated studies (e.g., by State Fish and Game) asserting it to be of critical importance."

On the other hand, "the legal arguments made by the intervenors were extremely strong," the report said. After citing the tidelands law in the constitution, the report concluded that "further argument would appear unnecessary... Lack of environmental inquiry, private domination of the bay, and use of tidelands for private residential purposes all violate established standards."

The New Board's Unanimous Vote

In a 1972 letter, Frank Robinson wrote, "We were fortunate in being able to elect two new members to the board of supervisors. The new board voted to cancel the tideland trade at their first meeting in January 1971... It's safe to say that Irvine domination of the county board of supervisors is greatly reduced at this moment in time. This was never considered possible in 'Irvine County.'" This meant that effectively the county no longer supported the proposed development of the bay.

Phil Berry's assistant Roger Hedgecock sent a Western Union telegram to the Robinsons on January 6, 1971, saying, "The supervisors vote is a victory for every Californian and a landmark in the battle for a livable environment. Irvine be hanged. Democracy lives in Newport Beach."

The New Coastal Commission

The Upper Newport Bay litigation was one of a number of legal challenges in the court system that led to California Proposition 20—the "Coastal Initiative"—appearing on the ballot in 1972. If Prop 20 passed, one state commission (the California Coastal Commission) and six regional commissions would oversee the use and development of California's coastline.

On November 7, 1972, Proposition 20 passed by an 800,000-vote margin despite opposition by business and labor interest, civic organizations, and most of California's major daily newspapers. Supporters were outspent by opponents nearly 100-to-1.

Proposition 20 author Peter Douglas—who would go on to direct the California Coastal Commission for 25 years—said, "After the initiative passed, speculative subdivisions came to a grinding halt." Investors realized the developments they had planned would not be approved, so they quickly sold the land to the State. Because of Prop 20, "there was a huge upswing in purchases of parks along the coast."

A New President for The Irvine Company

William R. Mason died of a heart attack at age 54 in 1973. Mason's successor, Raymond L. Watson, realized his company needed to "work with the regulatory bodies rather than fighting them as developers had commonly done," Martin A. Brower wrote in *Irvine Ranch: A Time for People.* "One of his first problems on becoming president in 1973 was to decide what to do with Upper Newport Bay."

"The Irvine Company, which had long been considered a good citizen of Orange County, had come out of the battle with a highly negative image," wrote Brower. "If the company was to get entitlement for other projects, Watson realized, the firm he now headed had to regain the public's favor."

—

By 1973, it seemed to the public as though The Irvine Company's marina was never going to happen. Of course, it wasn't as simple as that. Everything about this case was complicated. To make things clear to supporters, the Orange County Foundation for the Preservation of Public Property released a statement titled, "What Is the Status of the Upper Newport Bay Tideland Lawsuit?" It said, "Recent newspaper coverage… quite reasonably has caused many people to think that the trade is dead, and the lawsuit withdrawn from the courts. Unfortunately, this is not true." The statement listed six major facts:

1. The Board of Supervisors voted unanimously to cancel the trade.
2. The Irvine Company filed a separate suit to force the county to go through with the exchange.
3. The county hired Herman Selvin to represent the county in the appeal and in the public access rights suit.
4. The county's new position is that the county no longer considers the trade in the public's best interest.
5. The intervenors' continued participation is vital because in the appellate court, Herman Selvin can only submit the same information as the county's previous attorney.
6. If the Owens ruling is not appealed, protection of public tidelands guaranteed in Article XV, Section 3 of the California Constitution, will have been eliminated.

In a letter from the Orange County Foundation for the Preservation of Public Property updating potential donors, Allan Beek wrote, "An analysis of Judge Claude Owens' superior court opinion in favor of The Irvine Company has convinced us that it must be overturned, not only to protect the upper bay, but because of the significance of this case to tideland law elsewhere in California and the nation. With court approval of this tideland trade as a precedent, it would be only a short while before developers, through trades for larger tideland parcels, would control all the waterfront of our scarce remaining bays and estuaries."

At appeal, no new evidence can be introduced. No witnesses are called. The attorneys submit written briefs and may, on some occasions, give a brief oral argument before the judges. The three-judge appellate court then reviews the record of the case as it was heard in the lower court and decides if the lower court's ruling was erroneous or if it should stand.

During the long appeals process, the Robinsons continued to work with Berry but did not have to show up in court or do more research. They continued to collect newspaper clippings on environmental topics, discuss politics at the start of each Friends Tour, and attend Friends of Newport Bay board meetings (sometimes even holding them at their house). Life went on with hope.

In their trial briefs, Herman Selvin, who represented the county auditor, concentrated on the constitutional issue, and Phil Berry the contractual and environmental issues. In response to Selvin and Berry's briefs, The Irvine Company filed a lengthy, more than 90-page brief. Half of the response was devoted to attacking the intervenors' environmental position.

In the intervenors' brief, Berry wrote, in part:

> The law cannot approve alienation—or what amounts here to a giveaway—of trust lands for strictly private development… Here a unique natural resource, capable of many diffuse public uses, is proposed to be given over to narrow private purposes… Lack of comprehensive planning has led to a proposal, pushed by a powerful local minority interest through somnambulant, inattentive, or apathetic public bodies, which will wreck the basic resource—even for the intended private purposes.
>
> It cannot be said that the actions of either the Legislature or the SLC [State Lands Commission] or the county (which fortunately has reversed itself) have been adequate to protect the public interest… We respectfully submit that this is a proper case for judicial intervention…
>
> The constitutional objections to this exchange proposal are overwhelming… The net result of this entirely one-sided proposal would be so utterly and completely outside the purposes for which the tidelands trust was originally established.
>
> This is a case of tremendous moment, not just because it may determine the fate of a great natural resource. It is a significant test of the legal process itself. The failure to satisfy the provisions of Chapter 2044 and the constitutional obligations is so plain and obvious to the public that affirmance of the ill-advised and prejudicial decision of the court below would substantially worsen the already shaky faith of the public in our legal process.
>
> We respectfully submit that the judgment should be reversed…

His brief was dated and signed by Phillip S. Berry, March 15, 1972.

Putting the Fun in Fundraising

In addition to writing letters, voting, and donating their time, bay supporters could give monetary support. Money specifically for the friendly lawsuit could be donated to the Orange County Foundation for the Preservation of Public Property. Trustee Allan Beek said, "Norton Simon, head of Hunt Foods, had one of his lawyers create the Foundation for us, which was a gift of some $10,000 to $15,000 of legal time. But he did come up with a godawful name!" Imagine what it was like to ask people to write a check out to the Orange County Foundation for the Preservation of Public Property!

Norton Simon was one of the many anonymous benefactors who helped the campaign; he never received any publicity for it. But today most Southern Californians know Norton Simon's name. Several years after helping the bay, the billionaire would find a home for his 4,000-object art collection in the Pasadena Museum of Modern Art, and in 1974 the museum was renamed the Norton Simon Museum.

While the decision was in the courts' hands, the Orange County Foundation for the Preservation of Public Property raised about $40,000, mainly from small donations from hundreds of individuals. Frances Robinson said, "We had donations from people way back on the East Coast. Somebody at Woods Hole [Massachusetts], for example, sent us $100. We didn't know this person… We got money from people in Hawaii; we got money from people in Alaska that we'll never see."

Although individuals were generous, the biggest moneymaker for the Foundation was a series of parties the Robinsons threw called Back Bay Bashes. Guests included faculty members from almost all the Orange County colleges; members of the Sierra Club, the Audubon society, Nature Conservancy, and Coastal Alliance; representatives from government agencies (including the

> Water Quality Control Board, the Orange County District Attorney's office, the Public Defender's office, and the EPA); and politicians (including mayors Ed Hirth and Don McInnis, and Senator Alan Cranston). Each party they threw netted about $4,000.
>
> Alan Remington brought his jazz combo. Fran would bake—often providing her famous Lemon Enchanted Cream Cake. Everyone would relax, have fun, and socialize. "We had many parties just for the fun of it," Frank Robinson said, "because a friendship bond combined with a principle bond for the preservation of the bay was the strongest thing I could ever think of… One of the things that held this group together so long was its common interest. We wanted open space. We wanted a beautiful place to live in and pass along to our kids."

A little over two years after the lower court decision, the appellate court announced its decision. The California State Lands Commission meeting minutes from June 28, 1973, stated, "On February 21, 1973, the District Court of Appeal, Fourth District, Second Division, reversed the trial court and declared that the Upper Newport Bay exchange violated Article XV, Section 3 of the California Constitution… The court ordered the judgment reversed and directed the trial court to deny the peremptory writ of mandate… The Court of Appeal decision stands and the case is closed."

————

The Irvine Company had two months to appeal the ruling and raise the decision to the California Supreme Court. On the final day it could have appealed, on April 2, 1973, the company said in a statement, "The Irvine Company still concurs in the legal views expressed to the courts by its attorneys and by the Attorney General on behalf of the State Lands Commission that the Upper Newport Bay land exchange is legal and constitutional. Nevertheless, the company believes that rather than continuing litigation on the constitutional and other issues, the interests of all concerned are better served by a fresh approach involving mutual and concerted efforts by public agencies and the company to achieve public ownership of the company's lands in Upper Newport Bay."

Fran Robinson would always remember the day she walked into a local restaurant and saw a newspaper headline announcing The Irvine Company's decision. She said, "I put a dime in the machine, took the paper to the table, and then down came the tears. The relief was so great, after 10 years."

The intervenors believed that The Irvine Company was told not to appeal the decision to the California Supreme Court, as it could potentially open up tidelands issues all over California. Up until 1976, the Lands Commission put together 140 to 150 similar trades that had gone through, Huntington Harbour being one of them. In the early 1960s in Huntington Beach, the Christiana Corporation dredged the Sunset Bay Estuary wetlands to build Huntington Harbour, and Frank suspected that this marina was seen as a prototype for Upper Newport Bay.

No matter the reason behind it, The Irvine Company finally relented.

A 1972 Financial Report from the Orange County Foundation for the Preservation of Public Property stated that Frank and Frances Robinson "spent between $4,000 and $5,000 in the years, beginning August 1963… Costs included hundreds of long-distance telephone calls, travel expense, a variety of stationery supplies and printing, mailing, babysitting in the early years, purchase of research materials, etc. They kept no record of these expenditures, which were not tax-deductible items until this Foundation came into existence…"

The Robinsons weren't the only ones to use their own bank accounts. The Foundation's report also stated, "Trustees Allan Beek and Dr. Charles Greening have contributed their own personal funds without requesting reimbursement. One particular donation by Allan Beek was the purchase of the transcript of the hearing before the State Lands Commission, a document urgently needed in our legal case."

As ordered by Fourth District Court of Appeal, The Irvine Company reimbursed some of the intervenors' court costs. They sent $5,127.55 to the Orange County Foundation for the Preservation of Public Property on June 4, 1973.

As a response to those asking what it cost to save the bay, a 1975 Orange County Foundation for the Preservation of Public Property financial report listed costs from 1963 to 1975, when the main legal battle was finally over. At the end of the brief financial statement, it said, "We conclude this citizen effort has cost approximately $65,000 since 1963." This included $30,000 in legal fees.

Phil Berry's best guess was that The Irvine Company had put in a quarter of a million to half a million dollars into the project. "And we beat them," said Frank, "with about $70,000. For every dollar we spent, it cost them a lot of money."

Paying Court Costs

Just because Phil Berry took the case at half his normal rate, that didn't mean fighting The Irvine Company in court was cheap. According to a financial report from the Orange County Foundation for the Preservation of Public Property, the Sierra Club also assumed some of Phillip Berry's costs, such as travel fare from Oakland to Orange County during the trial, and costs of Roger Hedgecock's legal assistance. Regardless, by 1972, Phil Berry was owed about $10,000 for his work.

"We didn't keep records of our personal expenditures for most of the [first] nine years," Frank said. "Our guess is that we spent somewhere between $4,000 and $5,000, none of which was tax-deductible until the Foundation was a reality in December 1969."

The Robinsons felt the government had not done its job to protect the citizens, and they gave up their own time and money to pick up the slack. In a December 18, 1969, letter from the Robinsons to the Assembly Committee on Natural Resources and Conservation in Sacramento, they wrote, "The fact that six individual citizens have had to intervene in this suit to protect the public interest, which should have been protected by the various branches of government, is dramatic and astonishing proof that our constitutional guarantees of access to the shore can be circumvented… We believe we have an excellent case and that we intervenors will win it. We also believe we ought to send the bills we are paying for legal fees to the legislature for reimbursement."

They were never reimbursed by the legislature, of course, but when the intervenors received donations from private individuals, they were grateful. In a 1971 thank-you letter to one donor, Frank and Fran wrote, "Your contribution made it possible to pay another large bill which arrived last week. Without your help, we would be in debt at this time. We still have to raise funds for the remainder of the court action, but we are confident that somehow we will manage this."

Part Three | Creating an Ecological Reserve

Chapter Seven

FINALLY A NATURE PARK

In 1972, a lot of work still needed to be done to save the bay. The land had to be transferred from The Irvine Company to an agency that would maintain the area, the buyer and seller needed to agree on a purchase price, and the local government had to sign off on how the land would be used.

For years, ideas had been thrown around as to what to do with the land. Chuck Greening, the first president of Friends of Newport Bay, said in a 1990 *Los Angeles Times* article that there had been "wildly divergent ideas" of what the park should be. One person wanted an amusement park-type miniature city. Another, because of recent fossil discoveries in the bay, wanted to preserve the area as a scientific and historical landmark similar to the La Brea tar pits. Others wanted the bay to be closed off to humans completely.

"By the time 1973 got around," Frank Robinson said, "it had already been determined what it was going to be." Most supporters wanted a nature park and reserve. "Clean it up a little bit, but don't do much with it," Frank said. "Just leave the damn thing alone is what people really wanted."

Because the Orange County Board of Supervisors would have to approve an ecological reserve, Chairman of the Board Ron Caspers said to Frank, "I'll put this before the board, but you better give us some letters of support."

Frank reached out to his network of bay supporters, and the board received 2,500 letters. Before that, the largest amount of letters they ever received on one topic was 100.

Frank said, "I got a call from them, and they said, 'Christ! Can you cut it out? We can't find our mail!' It screwed up the whole place for two weeks, but the message got across. It was unanimously voted."

The land would be an ecological reserve, but they still had to secure the land itself.

———

In August 1973, The Irvine Company met with the State Department of Fish and Game. The department was interested in purchasing the land from The Irvine Company. In early 1974, G. Ray Arnett, director of the California Department of Fish and Game, and The Irvine Company President Raymond L. Watson signed a "Memorandum of Understanding." They agreed "that it would be in their mutual interests to arrive at a method by which the public can acquire ownership of those portions of Upper Newport Bay… although funds are not immediately available for such acquisition." The parties agreed to define the land to be acquired, appraise the land, and agree on a purchase price. The lands would be parceled, each given a price, and all parcels would be paid for within 10 years. For those 10 years The Irvine Company would "have no right of entry or right to use the lands beyond those rights normally afforded the general public upon said lands." The Department of Fish and Game would also receive a preliminary title report and a policy of title insurance. The memo also states that the deal was contingent on settling the suit Orange County had brought against The Irvine Company regarding public access rights in and around Upper Newport Bay.

Before the purchase price was settled, the Upper Newport Bay Ecological Reserve was dedicated at a ceremony on April 11, 1975, 12 years after the fight began. Meanwhile, dollar estimates of Upper Newport Bay's three islands were coming in as low as $118,000 to as high as $12 million, with each side having wildly different expectations of what was to be paid. According to the June 23, 1972, issue of *Los Angeles Times,* William R. Mason called the proposed purchase prices "utterly ridiculous." One month after the appellate court's ruling, The Irvine Company had offered to sell 527 acres (the three islands and some shoreline to the public) for $27.5 million, but their price eventually was reduced to $3.418 million.

The presumed reason why The Irvine Company came down so much on the price was because of that lawsuit from the County of Orange regarding prescriptive rights.

"There is a law in California," Ray Williams, president of the Friends in the 1970s said. "If the public has, over a period of years, become accustomed to passing through private property to get to public property and the private landowner has made no effort to block it, then the public may, in fact, have established the right to continue to do so." Over a period of two years, 1,500 signed affidavits were collected from people who had accessed the bay through lands claimed by The Irvine Company, some for as long as 50 years.

Allan Beek, trustee of the Orange County Foundation for the Preservation of Public Property, said, "Frank was entertained that one of the people who reported what they had used the land for was 'to lose my virginity!'"

Ray Williams said, "There appeared to be enough evidence to actually make a public claim to the lands involved and get them for free if the company contested the prescriptive rights in court. They settled without going to court for the $3.418 million. [This money] came out of a penalty fund set up after the [1969] Santa Barbara oil disaster into which the oil companies paid. Thus, no tax money was used." The Irvine Company would also pay Orange County $1.65 million for disputed back taxes.

In 1975 the state legislature voted unanimously to pay The Irvine Company the $3.418 million and to give control over to the Department of Fish and Game to operate the park within its ecological reserve system. Governor Jerry Brown signed SB368 on September 15, 1975, which appropriated the money for the 527 acres in and around Upper Newport Bay, assuring a permanent reserve of 741 total acres.

It wasn't over yet. The dollar amount was agreed upon, money allocated, the land approved for a park, and the reserve dedicated. But the Friends, Orange County Foundation for the Preservation of Public Property, the Sierra Club, and especially Frank Robinson were still not completely satisfied.

A few years later, as Penelope Moffet explained in the June 1979 issue of *Orange County Illustrated*, "the Robinsons and three other individuals (Allan Beek, Jean E. Cohen, and Michele Perrault) joined with the Orange County Foundation for the Preservation of Public Property and the Sierra Club to not-so-quietly drop a complaint into the county clerk's lap [in April 1979]. The complaint states that California's 1975 purchase of 527 acres of bayshore property islands in Upper Newport Bay, land which now forms part of a 741-acre ecological reserve, was illegal. It asks that the $3.5 million spent to buy that land be returned."

The case rested upon the plaintiffs proving that the islands were originally tidelands when California became a state in 1850.

In a 1975 letter, Frank Robinson explained how they came to this conclusion. "Near the end of the court trial in 1971," Frank said, "we started to investigate the title to the Irvine islands in UNB. Up to this point in time, I had assumed that the title was clear and unencumbered. As our investigation progressed, more and more evidence started to accumulate to the effect that the islands were in fact tidelands as of 1850—the time when California joined the Union… The 1850 date is very important since that is the date when the state assumed the common law trust over the tidelands. It is the conditions as of 1850 that determine the boundary between the tidelands and the uplands held in private ownership. Starting in 1855, the state legislature began selling tidelands to individuals throughout the state. This practice continued for 54 years until 1909 when the legislature passed a law forbidding any further sale of state tidelands. During those 54 years, the state sold tidelands which were identified (erroneously) as 'swamp and overflow land.'"

Pointing to a survey conducted in 1889, Frank said that in the original notes of the survey, the islands were identified as tidelands. These notes, Frank said, "were changed and the 'swamp and overflow' term was substituted for 'tidelands' in a different handwriting… Our UNB investigation revealed that past State Lands Commissions have given away thousands of acres of priceless tidelands." Many other maps and documents supported Frank's position (see "Another Map Found" on next page).

Lane Koluvek, president of Friends of Newport Bay, said, "We wanted The Irvine Company to give back the money they were paid for [the three islands]." But Frank and Fran "saw the writing on the wall; they would never win because others saw that it would cause too much upheaval in lands up and down the state, that property in private hands would have to revert to the state."

The Irvine Company's response to Frank's complaint was, "We're not terribly alarmed." Jerry Collins, associate director of public relations, said that when the company sold the land at one-sixth of its assessed value, everyone applauded. "This apparent turnaround in their sentiments is baffling and disappointing. In any event, we fully expect the complaint to be dismissed." In 1987, a judge ruled in favor of The Irvine Company.

For the rest of his life, Frank believed the state should have gotten the land for free, but, he said, "the state's not about to question the title to these basic lands when they've blessed 140 of these trades up and down the state. That would put, for instance, Huntington Harbour in question. Half the property there is on tidelands."

Another Map Found

Many maps and surveys throughout the years documented the Upper Newport Bay's changing shape, but one map made headlines. It was discovered in 1974 in Los Angeles when the State Lands Commission moved offices. A commission official found it when he was searching for an old map to hang on the bare walls of his new office.

A November 1974 *Orange County Register* article said, "A nearly 100-year-old map which officials say raises questions about The Irvine Company's ownership of valuable Upper Newport Bay land surfaced Tuesday as county supervisors concluded an agreement that will convert the bay into a wildlife sanctuary... Sources said Tuesday the 1878 map done by a former Los Angeles County surveyor before Orange County was formed could throw The Irvine Company back into court if the state claims those lands, some of which have been developed into housing tracts, or could result in a lower price on the ecological reserve."

Frances Robinson underlined the following quote from County Supervisor Robert Battin on her clipping of this article and wrote "Right on!" in the margin: "If The Irvine Company does not own the islands, we are today rushing to accommodate ourselves to a deal between the state and The Irvine Company to allow the public to pay for lands the public already owns." Battin was the only supervisor who opposed the county settlement in a 4-1 vote the Tuesday before.

Chapter Eight

FULL-TIME ATTENTION

~∽~

Frank Robinson always said, "You can never win a conservation battle, but you can always lose it. Because as long as it's open, it's subject to abuse. To preserve it takes full-time attention." Even though the Upper Newport Bay Ecological Reserve was a reality, that didn't mean the work was done. The bay would require constant attention and vigilance. The Robinsons had a lot going on after the park was dedicated in order to ensure that it could remain a viable estuary.

To Frank's chagrin, The Irvine Company never had to pay back the $3.418 million. He lost that battle, but a small victory was on the horizon. In the late 1980s, The Irvine Company would eventually donate 114 acres of still-undeveloped land surrounding the bay at a time when nearby land sold for $1 million an acre.

Back in 1974, Frank was quoted as saying in the *Los Angeles Times,* "We need every damn acre we can get." This included a buffer between the reserve and any commercial or residential development The Irvine Company might build on its remaining bayside lands. The upland area provides habitat for animals and plants that keep the other areas of the bay ecologically balanced. In that same *Los Angeles Times* article, President Raymond Watson said, The Irvine Company "is not averse to selling the uplands. But I hope they don't become transformed into a battleground."

It did not become a battleground, as both sides believed they reached an amicable solution. A partner group of the Friends of Newport Bay called Stop Polluting Our Newport (SPON) led the negotiations. SPON (now known as Still Protecting Our Newport) was born after a group of citizens watched as a torrential rainstorm in 1974 filled Upper Newport Bay with inland trash and other debris. Jean Watt and Claudia Hirsch led a group of activists to fight pollution, the expansion of John Wayne Airport, excess traffic, loss of open space, and other threats to Newport Beach's environment. In 1988, SPON sued the city of Newport Beach for its vote to allow The Irvine Company's expansion of Fashion Island even though it was not permitted by the city's general plan. SPON opposed the new development.

The deal was that in exchange for a donation of 114 acres of land, SPON agreed to drop its lawsuit, and The Irvine Company could begin expanding its Fashion Island shopping complex.

Allan Beek said that he, Terry Watt (Jean Watt's daughter), and a lawyer went to negotiate with Gary Hunt, the president The Irvine Company at the time. "It was really amicable," he said. "We could see they realized that the land they had wasn't very good for housing development [because it was under the airport flight path], and we realized that they could have the city council amend the general plan and get their expansion eventually. We both saw we could make a deal, and we did. They gave us the land, and we backed off… Everyone came out pretty satisfied."

Even though everyone said they were satisfied, The Irvine Company had a different story regarding the motive behind the donation. According to the July 19, 1989, issue of the *Orange County Register,* a spokesperson for The Irvine Company "denied there was any tradeoff involved and said the park was a 'gift to the people of Orange County.'" The spokesperson said that the park was "a spectacular piece of property that was worth a gold mine for residential development."

In 1989, 15 years from when the fight started for the bluffs and 25 years after the fight for the bay began, the bluffs were finally turned over to the county, and a ceremony was held overlooking the bay. Years later, Frances wrote in her scrapbook page showing photos from the dedication of the Upper Newport Bay Regional Park, "On July 25, 1989, there was jubilation at the dedication celebrating the transfer of 114 acres of uplands adjacent to Upper Newport Bay, from The Irvine Company to the County of Orange. According to the agreement, the county will restrict use of the land, named Upper Newport Bay Regional Park, to passive-type activities compatible with Upper Newport Bay State Ecological Reserve… There are 142 acres in the park which include the northern strip, the bluffs adjacent to Back Bay Road, and 65 acres on the west bay."

Reciprocal Support

Over the years, more environmental groups formed and supported the Friends of Newport Bay. Some groups needed support from the Friends. In the 1970s and '80s, a group called Amigos de Bolsa Chica fought to preserve wetlands in Huntington Beach, just a few miles north of Upper Newport Bay. The Amigos duplicated the Friends' strategy by lobbying politicians and bringing several lawsuits against developer Signal Landmark, which proposed building 5,000 to 10,000 homes on the wetlands. They settled with Signal in 1989 and formed the 1,300-acre Bolsa Chica Ecological Reserve. The Friends' experience also helped Friends of Ballona Wetlands, about 50 miles north of Upper Newport Bay. In 1984, this group filed a lawsuit against the California Coastal Commission after development plans were approved. The lawsuit was settled in 1990, saving 340 acres. Ballona is the largest remaining wetlands area in Los Angeles County. Advice from the Robinsons also made Crescent Bay Point Park in Laguna Beach possible. Nonprofits that have supported Upper Newport Bay include SPON (Stop Polluting Our Newport) founded in 1974, Defend the Bay founded in 1995, Friends of Harbors, Beaches and Parks founded in 1996, and O.C. Coastkeepers founded in 1999.

In the 1990s, the Friends of Newport Bay and the Upper Newport Bay Naturalists, led by Jack Keating, were busy fundraising for an interpretive center. Frances always believed that the bay would be saved forever if there was a building there dedicated to teaching people about it. Around 1975, Fran mentioned this dream of hers to Chuck Greening. Chuck reportedly had said, "Oh, Fran! That's 25 years in the future!" At the interpretive center's dedication in 2000, Fran reproved Chuck for his lack of accuracy, saying, "Chuck, you missed it by three months!"

Fran had an interpretive center in mind years before her conversation with Chuck. As early as 1971 architect Ron Yeo was bicycling around the bay to research potential center sites to realize Fran's dream, but he could not begin building for another 27 years.

Finally, in the 1990s, to make the interpretive center a reality, The Irvine Company gave another 14 acres of its bayfront land to the county, Newport Beach donated 6 acres of its land, and the county allocated some money (from a private donation) for the center's construction.

The center is named after Peter and Mary Muth, who generously gave $1 million to the Orange County parks department. For more than 50 years, the Muths had owned Orco Block. Inc., a Stanton manufacturer and seller of concrete blocks. Peter Muth said, "Mary and I are thankful for our success in Orange County, and we want to leave something for the future, and we felt a donation to the parks department was the correct place to put it." At the time of their donation, Peter Muth told Supervisor Thomas Riley, "It's there when the right thing comes along."

Supervisor Tom Wilson, who represented Newport Beach, proposed naming the center after Peter and Mary Muth, and the name was approved by Orange County leaders. An exhibit hall inside would be named after the Robinsons.

In the *Daily Pilot,* Frank said of the Muths, "They gave what they had, the money. And we gave what we had, the energy and time." The Robinsons and the Muths had known each other since the late 1970s, when they met at a ballroom dancing club the couples belonged to in Santa Ana.

In the April-June 2000 issue of the Friends of Newport Bay newsletter, called *TRACKS,* Park Ranger Nancy Bruland wrote, "The interpretive center was officially named the Peter and Mary Muth Interpretive Center… What gave this park ranger the greatest joy, though, was the official naming of the Exhibit Hall—The Frank and Frances Robinson Exhibit Hall. No two people have put more blood, sweat, and tears into protecting Upper Newport Bay than Frank and Fran Robinson."

Bob Caustin, founder of another Newport Beach environmental organization called Defend the Bay, said, "I'd like to see the whole thing named after Frank and Fran—without them, the whole thing would be homes and docks. It was incredible vision they had, and it's wonderful they are seeing this in their lifetime."

With the money secured and the land at the northern end of the park (at the corner of University Drive and Irvine Avenue) donated, architect Ron Yeo could finalize his plans. Yeo, who started his own full-time architectural practice in Corona del Mar in 1962 and served two times as an Orange County Planning Commissioner, had big plans for the center.

His firm, which did architectural work for at least 10 parks throughout Southern California, as well as Pier Plaza in Huntington Beach, was known for environmentally friendly designs. In the early design stages, Yeo and his associate Patrick Marr wanted to see if they could develop a structure using only waste products directly from the bay. They made bricks from mud in the bay that needed to be dredged anyway, but that type of building would have been too tall for the site. And, after a loss of public funds when the county went bankrupt in 1994, the plan of a completely subterranean building had to be significantly scaled back, with the building jutting out of the cliff instead. "Cost-wise, we could only do half of what we envisioned," Yeo said in the *Los Angeles Times*. "That was a little disappointing."

They instead used concrete made from sand, gravel, and water from upstream riverbeds along Aliso and Trabuco Creeks. They reinforced the concrete with rebar made from 2,400 pounds of confiscated firearms from 27 Southern California law enforcement agencies, 362,400 pounds of used oil filters, 228,000 pounds of steel-belted tire cords, and 7,200 pounds of steel drums and containers. The doors were laminated with scraps of leftover mahogany that would have been thrown away, bathroom countertops were made from recycled glass and tile, and the carpets were made from 7,000 post-consumer plastic bottles. The green roof of the 10,000-square-foot building lies even with the parking lot, and the building cannot be seen from street-level. Yeo explained in the *Los Angeles Times*, "We wanted to preserve as much open space as possible, so we tucked it underneath."

Construction was supposed to begin in 1997. Frank mentioned the interpretive center in the newsletter *TRACKS*. "After many starts and stops due to the county bankruptcy, severe soil problems, excessive cost estimates, and archeological finds, we are happy to report that construction plans for the nature center are back on track... Groundbreaking ceremonies are scheduled for January (our wettest month) 1997. Hope to see you all there, and be sure to bring an umbrella." The rain did come, and unfortunately it also prevented the start of construction.

After more delays, construction finally began in June 1998, and the building took two years to complete. The interpretive center finally opened on October 14, 2000, with a celebration that included food, live and silent auctions, personal tours of all hands-on exhibits, and live musical entertainment.

The center would provide a visitor experience of the bay through exhibits and interactive displays on the Upper Newport Bay estuary. In the October 14, 2000, issue of the *Orange County Register,* Jack Keating said, "The center is important because people need to know how important the bay is, how it's used by animals, birds, and plants. What the threats are: trash, sediments, excessive nutrients, pathogens."

"When you put half a lifetime into something, there's not a big enough batch of superlatives to describe your joy," Frank said. The opening of the interpretive center was "the happiest day of my life, with the exception of the day Frances and I married."

Much-Deserved Recognition

In addition to the interpretive center's Frank and Frances Robinson Exhibit Hall, the Robinsons were recognized for their work with numerous national, state, and local awards, including awards from the Audubon Society and American Motors. At the Sierra Club Annual Banquet in May 1974, their lawyer Philip Berry presented Frank and Fran with honorary life membership to the Sierra Club. Frances was named alumna of the year at Fremont High School for her efforts in environmental causes.

Even Ray Watson, former president of The Irvine Company, nominated the Robinsons for an award from the American Institute of Architects' California chapter. (Like the Robinsons, Watson was a busy man during his lifetime. In addition to his work at The Irvine Company, he was on the board at Walt Disney Productions from 1972 until his retirement in 2004. He died in 2012 at age 86. He and his wife, Elsa, donated money to the Upper Newport Bay cause, and the theater in the Peter and Mary Muth Interpretive Center is named after them.)

Chapter Nine

REFLECTIONS ON THE 25-YEAR BATTLE

On June 30, 2001, less than a year after her dream interpretive center opened, Frances Robinson died of congestive heart failure in her home at 1007 Nottingham Road, Newport Beach. Fran had done some gardening and took a swim in her pool that day, and then lay down because she felt tired.

Fran was 82 and had been married to Frank for 59 years.

Upper Newport Bay took up a lot of her time, but Fran was much more than a woman who fought to preserve the bay. She was a wife, mother, friend, gardener, photographer and videographer, swimmer, water-skier, ballroom dancer, and traveler. "Frances was 72 when she and Frank went on a tour to Ecuador and the Galapagos Islands," said the *Orange County Register* the week following her death. "They were the oldest members of the group, and Frances astounded everyone by plunging into the ocean to swim with the seals."

The greatest joy of her life, Fran had said, was her mother taking her to the beach when she was a young girl. She loved the water. "She had to be in the water every day," said friend Linda Koluvek, whether it be dipping her toes into the bay during a beach barbecue party at North Star Beach, water skiing at Lake Powell while on vacation, or swimming in her backyard pool. It is a comfort to know she felt the joy of swimming at her Newport Beach home on the last day of her life.

More than 200 people gathered at the Peter and Mary Muth Interpretive Center for her memorial service on Thursday, July 5. On that drizzly morning, many people shared their fond memories of

Frances Robinson. Bob Caustin, founder of Defend the Bay, said that Fran "dedicated a tremendous amount of her life to the public benefit." He motioned toward the bay behind him and said, "This would have been a housing tract."

Her son, Jay, said that she had lost much of her memory after a heart attack four years before, and it had saddened him to see her health deteriorate since that time.

"When they were building the Muth Center," Fran's friend Linda Koluvek said, "every day Frank would take her to see it, and every day it was a brand-new experience… Frank had the biggest thrill by showing it to her… That was the best thing he could do."

In Upper Newport Bay's October-December 2001 *TRACKS* newsletter, Upper Newport Bay volunteer and board member Amy Litton said, "Fran's legacy was to ensure that we would all have access to the 'Back Bay' and that the plants, animals, and habitat we all know to be so important, would be protected in perpetuity… As you stroll through the nature reserve, ride a bike along the San Diego Creek trail, or join in on a weekend canoe or kayak tour, remember her determination and spirit that contributed so much to all you're enjoying. She will be deeply missed but never forgotten."

After Fran's passing, Frank—then affectionately called "the fossil of the bay"—wanted to create a memorial for Frances. He worked with the interpretive center's architect Ron Yeo and Jim Cokas, one of the members of the new naturalist class in 1990. The memorial would be located at Vista Point, the starting point for the Friends Tours since 1968, at the corner of Back Bay Drive and Eastbluff Drive.

Frank's health had been in decline since Fran's passing. He had suffered a stroke as well. He died in his sleep two years after Fran on April 10, 2003, at age 84, before Fran's memorial could be completed. His memorial service was also held at the Muth Center.

In the June-August 2003 issue of *TRACKS*, volunteer Amy Litton thanked Frank for his impact. She wrote, "We have all benefited from the fruits of your labor. I shudder to think what might have happened to our bay if you had not married Frances or moved to Newport Beach in 1962; had you not made the decision to follow through when your son reported that access to the bay was being restricted, instead of shrugging it off… Thank you for having the spunk, the intelligence, and the congenial personality that converted many skeptics during a time when others passed on helping because a battle appeared to be lost. The tide turned, didn't it? As you'd hoped it would… In a time before we celebrated an 'Earth Day,' you demonstrated so beautifully how to effect change within the system by immersing yourself in the process... Thank you for showing us how a few volunteers can transform the world we live in... Each year new volunteers join seasoned veterans... The ones who join next year, and from now on, will not have the pleasure of meeting you, Frank, and seeing that smile, or hearing one of the many jokes you often shared. But they will have the pleasure of helping to preserve Upper Newport Bay. Your spirit lives on, Frank, in ways too numerous to count. Thank you for sharing your journey with us in so many ways and for so long. We'll miss you."

Jim Cokas, who was working on Fran's memorial, was able to show Frank a miniature model of the yet-to-be constructed Vista Point before he passed away. "He still had that great smile and bright eyes," Cokas told the *Daily Pilot*. "Just seeing that full-sized smile spread across his face was really gratifying."

"We had met with the intent for a memorial to Frances," Cokas said, "but it became clear the memorial really had to be for both of them." So, Vista Point was formally dedicated to Frank and Frances Robinson on November 8, 2008. The overlook provides a stunning view of the bay, amphitheater seating, visitor information, viewing scopes, interpretive panels, and a small monument dedicated to the Robinsons. A quote from anthropologist Margaret Mead is featured on the memorial: "Never doubt that a small group of thoughtful, committed citizens can change the world. Indeed, it is the only thing that ever has."

Frank and Fran were thoughtful. They were certainly committed. And they really did change the world. Chuck Greening, first president of the Friends of Newport Bay, once said, "Who could take on The Irvine Company, the city of Newport Beach, the county, and the newspapers, and win? But they did. I have never seen anyone work so long and hard and intensively for a cause as the Robinsons. Both of them. Frank and Fran. You can't separate them."

———

Had it not been for the Robinsons' intervention, today Upper Newport Bay would be a navigable waterway filled with boats. According to the approved "Upper Newport Bay Land Exchange Plan," dated March 31, 1964, at the north end of the bay there would be a mile-long rowing course and a marine stadium separated by a long, narrow strip of public park land with a swimming beach. North of the marine stadium would be another public park with boat-launching facilities.

On the east side of the bay would be a 67-acre public park, and on the west side, the public would have access to just two small parks, each less than 5 acres and just 400 to 600 feet of beach. The southeast side would have a public park with a swimming lagoon and boat-launching facilities (about 70 acres), but this was already publicly owned land. The remaining land would be Irvine-owned and filled with homes, businesses, and private boat basins.

Imagine the tranquil Upper Newport Bay resembling today's congested lower bay and Balboa Island, which was developed in the 1920s and '30s by removing sandbars and building marshlands into islands. Even though the upper bay was not developed, the lower bay is still "the largest pleasure harbor in the nation," according to the January 1, 2000, issue of the *Daily Pilot,* "docking more than 9,000 watercraft."

Today Upper Newport Bay is open to everyone, not just the privileged few. Visitors can enjoy more than 1,000 acres of open space, with walking, jogging, kayaking, and bicycling opportunities—a rare luxury in such a densely populated urban area. The bay serves as an outdoor classroom for more than 10,000 local school children each year and is a delight for thousands of birdwatchers. And, maybe most importantly, the bay, which is the largest of just a few remaining natural estuaries in Southern California, provides an ecologically balanced home to unique flora and fauna too numerous to count.

"For us it started in 1963," Frank said. "From there it was like a stone dropped into water; the rings spread, getting bigger and bigger and bigger. We were a small group up against the big guys."

Standing up against the big guys meant a lot of work, even after the main battle was won. In a 1992 interview with historian James A. Aldridge, Frances said that in retirement Frank had become such a popular speaker that he was "speaking himself to death." There was burnout among a lot of the original bay supporters. "Most of us are worked to death… You just get tired after a while. How we've kept it up for 29 years, I just don't know."

Because the Robinsons gained so much expertise over the years, Frank became a Harbors, Parks and Beaches commissioner in the 1970s, ensuring that Dana Point Harbor would not be restricted to wealthy boaters. Frances was asked to be a participant in a Department of the Interior task force that studied if Upper Newport Bay could remain a viable estuary despite rapid urbanization in the watershed. "I worked like a dog for two months, really burned the midnight oil every night," she said.

Through all the years, the Robinsons remained closely involved with the Friends, hosting board meetings at their home, fundraising, talking at Friends Tours, writing articles for the Upper Newport Bay newsletter, and doing anything else they could to preserve the bay for future generations.

When asked if it was all worth it, Fran exclaimed, "Of course it's been worth it!" Her greatest reward—her "blessing," she called it—was meeting an elementary school child who thanked her for saving the bay. "What could be a greater reward than that?" Frances said. "There is none."

Afterword

UPPER NEWPORT BAY TODAY

~⌇~

"You can never win a conservation battle, but you can always lose it," Frank Robinson had said. "Because as long as it's open, it's subject to abuse, but to preserve it takes full-time attention." Since the Robinsons passed, Upper Newport Bay has been subject to a lot of abuse, including unintended effects from nearby development, water contamination, sedimentation, trespassing, invasive non-native plants, and much more.

But dedicated people have helped keep the bay as healthy as possible. There have been many other battles and many victories throughout the years, including blocking the expansion of the nearby University Drive, preventing waste water from being dumped into the bay, constructing the Back Bay Science Center in 2008, and making headway in habitat restoration.

More than 200 regular volunteers contribute more than 10,000 hours per year, greeting visitors at the front desk of the Peter and Mary Muth Interpretive Center, restoring the bay's habitat, leading guided walking and kayak tours, educating school groups, fundraising, and much more. Thousands of one-time volunteers aid in habitat restoration or trash removal during corporate events or those organized by bay volunteers and staff, such as the Coastal Cleanup Day event each September. Staff from the Newport Bay Conservancy, Orange County Parks, the city of Newport Beach, and the California Department of Fish and Wildlife (previously known as California Department of Fish and Game until 2013) work together to run day-to-day operations and organize special events.

You don't have to work or volunteer at Upper Newport Bay to continue the Robinsons' legacy. Visit the bay for a guided walking or kayaking tour, or stroll with your family at your own pace along any of the walking trails. Explore the Peter and Mary Muth Interpretive Center to learn more about what you can find in the bay. Choose your favorite painting from a plein air art exhibition held at the bay and hang it in your home. Drive, bike, or walk Back Bay Drive. Get "hands-on" with the touch tanks at the Back Bay Science Center, which sits on Shellmaker Island. Launch your kayak from the Newport Aquatic Center on North Star Beach, where Jay Robinson found The Irvine Company's "Private Property" sign. Bring binoculars and count all the different bird species you see. Have fun trying to identify them while keeping an eye open for jumping fish! And take in the view at Vista Point, where the Friends of Newport Bay launched their Friends Tours more than 50 years ago.

When you're back at home, share your experiences with your friends. If you want to do more, visit www.newportbay.org to see how you can donate money or volunteer your time. You can also volunteer at the bay or other open space areas in Orange County through The Irvine Company's nonprofit and Newport Bay Conservancy partner, the Irvine Ranch Conservancy (www.irconservancy.org). This organization, founded in 2005, works to protect and restore the natural resources of nearly 40,000 acres of open space on the historic Irvine Ranch.

Write to politicians just like Frances Robinson did and urge them to protect natural areas like Upper Newport Bay. Stay informed. And keep the idea of public access with you wherever you go, knowing that in an urban environment, open spaces are vital escapes for nearby residents.

Because of the Robinsons and the thousands of other people who have fought for Upper Newport Bay over the years (even in a small way, like reading a book about the subject!) there is hope for the bay's future. While there are still people who care, the battle to preserve the bay will continue to be won.

References

Saving the Bay Timeline

1962. The Robinson family (Frank, Frances, Jay, and Dana) moves from La Cañada to 1007 Nottingham Road, Newport Beach.

1963. Jay Robinson discovers The Irvine Company's "Private Property" signs on North Star Beach, several blocks away from the Robinson home.

1963. Frances Robinson's letter to the editor is published in the *Daily Pilot*, and the public awareness campaign begins. Citizens begin to learn about the proposed land trade between Orange County and The Irvine Company, and the plans to develop Upper Newport Bay into a marina.

1964-65. The city of Newport Beach, Orange County Board of Supervisors, Orange County Harbor District, and The Irvine Company work out the details on the plan for Upper Newport Bay.

1965. Recently elected to the Orange County Board of Supervisors, Robert Battin opposes the land trade. Politicians in Sacramento also become concerned about the legality of the trade.

1966. The State Lands Commission turns down the land trade proposal as not in the public interest, telling The Irvine Company to revise the plan.

1967. Dr. Judy B. Rosener writes the Orange County Grand Jury report, which cites the exchange's enormous disadvantages to the public.

1967. Community members set up an organization called Friends of Newport Bay, with the first meeting in the fall of 1967, after environmental positions were not taken seriously at the State Lands Commission hearing concerning the land trade.

1968. Friends of Newport Bay begins hosting educational Friends Tours, which attract hundreds of people to Upper Newport Bay each month.

1969. The devastating Santa Barbara oil spill in January and February kicks off the environmentalist movement.

1969. *Sunset Magazine* highlights the citizen campaign and Friends Tours. The exposure brings nearly 1,000 people to the next Friends Tour, which is held in the pouring rain.

1969. Orange County Foundation for the Preservation of Public Property is founded to fund the legal fight against the land trade.

1969. Wesley and Judith Marx, Harold and Joan Coverdale, and Frank and Frances Robinson petition to act as intervenors in the friendly lawsuit between Orange County and The Irvine Company.

1970. Trial begins in June and lasts for six weeks. Judge Claude A. Owens rules the trade constitutional. The intervenors file for appeal, and the County of Orange brings a separate lawsuit against The Irvine Company.

1971. The Ralph Nader Task Force publishes a report called "Power and Land in California," which criticizes the proposed land trade and emphasizes the ecological importance of the bay.

1971-72. The U.S. Department of the Interior Task Force on Upper Newport Bay is established. Frances Robinson is invited to be one of two local participants.

1972. An article in the October issue of *TIME* magazine called "Saving the West" drew national attention to Upper Newport Bay.

1973. The California appeals court reverses Judge Claude A. Owens' decision and rules the land trade unconstitutional.

1975. Upper Newport Bay Ecological Reserve is dedicated on April 11.

1975. A purchase price for land owned by The Irvine Company is agreed upon, and the land is turned over to the State Department of Fish and Game.

1979. The Orange County Foundation for the Preservation of Public Property files a lawsuit for the return of $3.48 million paid to The Irvine Company for the land, plus interest, citing that the company did not own the land to begin with.

1987. Judge Judith Ryan rules in favor of The Irvine Company, meaning the company keeps the $3.48 million paid for the land.

1990. The Irvine Company, in exchange for development rights for Fashion Island, gives Orange County 114 acres of bluffs and grasslands around the bay for a regional park.

1998. Construction on the Peter and Mary Muth Interpretive Center begins.

2000. The interpretive center opens to the public.

2008. The Back Bay Science Center and Vista Point open.

2012. All of Upper Newport Bay down to the Pacific Coast Highway bridge is designated as a State Marine Conservation Area, not just the Ecological Reserve.

Key People Who Saved the Bay

Baldwin, Charles. Special investigator for the State Tidelands Committee who visited the Robinsons and early bay supporters to look at the proposed land trade between Orange County and The Irvine Company.

Battin, Robert. First member of the Orange County Board of Supervisors (elected 1965) to oppose the land exchange.

Beek, Allan. One of the three trustees of Orange County Foundation for the Preservation of Public Property, the legal defense fund for the intervenors in the friendly lawsuit with The Irvine Company. Beek testified at the friendly lawsuit and was one of 27 named sponsors of the Upper Newport Bay Defense Fund. He has been a member (since 1980) and secretary (since 1985) of SPON. SPON helped secure 114 additional acres for Upper Newport Bay Ecological Reserve in 1990.

Berry, Phil. President of the Sierra Club and trial attorney from Oakland, who represented the Robinsons and other intervenors in the 1970 lawsuit.

Caspers, Ronald. Elected to the Orange County Board of Supervisors with the Robinsons' help. He was vocal about saving the bay, and he also voted to purchase 5,500 acres of open space for an Orange County park. The park was named after him in 1974 after Caspers died in office when he and nine of his family and friends died at sea when their boat *Shooting Star* sank off the coast of Baja California.

Coverdale, Harold and Joan. Joint intervenors in the friendly lawsuit with The Irvine Company with Wesley and Judith Marx, and Frank and Frances Robinson.

Gilbertson, Lance. Biologist and Upper Newport Bay volunteer who manned the "Mud Stop" on the Friends Tours. He would later discover two new land snail species along the U.S.-Mexico border.

Greening, Charles. One of the three trustees of Orange County Foundation for the Preservation of Public Property. He was an engineer and physicist with a Ph.D. in Educational Psychology who helped set up the Friends of Newport Bay. He served as president for eight years and on the board for 20 years, and manned the "Bird Stop" on the Friends Tours. Chuck testified at the friendly lawsuit, providing details about Friends Tours and visitors to the bay.

Hall, Robert. One of the three trustees of Orange County Foundation for the Preservation of Public Property, the legal defense fund for the intervenors.

Hedgecock, Roger. Law student who assisted Phil Berry with the 1970 lawsuit.

Heim, V.A. Orange County auditor who refused to reimburse The Irvine Company for certain engineering costs on their early work in the bay. His refusal to pay was one of the reasons for the friendly lawsuit.

Hinshaw, Andrew J. Orange County assessor in the 1960s who later became a congressman. An early critic of the land exchange, he was often quoted in the papers as saying the assessed values of The Irvine Company lands were too low and that the exchange did not benefit the public. He testified at the friendly lawsuit in 1970.

Hirsch, Claudia. One of the co-founders of SPON.

Johns, Buck. Was instrumental in Frank Robinson's fight to block the extension of nearby University Drive into a four-to-six-lane highway in the late 1980s.

Keating, Jack. Aerospace engineer and Newport Beach resident who moved to his home in 1964 initially wanting the bay to be developed into a pleasure harbor. Because of the Robinsons' public education, he changed his mind and became involved with Upper Newport Bay as a volunteer. He served as president of Upper Newport Bay Naturalists and Newport Bay Naturalists and Friends for 10 years. He was a major fundraiser for the Peter and Muth Interpretive Center and later, the Back Bay Science Center.

Koluvek, Lane. Close friend of the Robinsons and president of Friends of Newport Bay for 12 years.

Koluvek, Linda. Close friend of the Robinsons and treasurer of Friends of Newport Bay.

Marx, Wesley and Judith. Joint intervenors with Frank and Frances Robinson, and Harold and Joan Coverdale in the friendly lawsuit with The Irvine Company. Wesley, as the writer of *Frail Ocean,* was the only intervenor to testify in court.

Mason, William. President of The Irvine Company from 1966 to 1973. He testified at the friendly lawsuit in 1970.

Muth, Peter and Mary. Owners of Orco Block, Inc. in Stanton, who donated $1 million to the Orange County Parks department. Their donation was used to fund the construction of Upper Newport Bay's interpretive center, which opened in 2000.

North, Dr. Wheeler James. Kelp forester and Caltech scientist who often testified as an environmental expert at hearings alongside Frank Robinson and who was often quoted in newspapers. He testified at the friendly lawsuit in 1970.

Owens, Claude A. Judge who presided over the friendly lawsuit in 1970. His decision that the land exchange was constitutional was reversed in 1973 by the appellate court.

Perry, Ralph. Sierra Club member and lawyer from Los Angeles, who was the Robinsons' first lawyer.

Robinson, Frances. Skilled writer and organizer, who, along with her husband, Frank, led the campaign to save Upper Newport Bay from development.

Robinson, Frank. Aerospace engineer who, along with his wife, Frances, analyzed documents, spoke at meetings and hearings, and organized the legal fight against the development of Upper Newport Bay.

Robinson, Jay. Son of Frank and Frances Robinson, who discovered The Irvine Company's "Private Property" sign on North Star Beach. Inspired by watching his parents fight The Irvine Company in court, he graduated from the University of California, Los Angeles, in 1972 and became an attorney.

Schneebeck, Chuck. California State University, Fullerton, professor whose biology students studied at the bay and often became volunteers. He educated many people at the university about the plight of the bay.

Unruh, Jesse. Leader of the California State Assembly and head of the State Tidelands Committee, which looked into the legality of the land trade early on in the fight to save the bay. Unruh was vocal about the trade not being in the public's best interest.

Watson, Raymond L. Vice president and then president of The Irvine Company from 1973 to 1977. He was a friend and neighbor of Jack Keating and became a supporter of the bay. The Muth Center's theater is named after him and his wife, Elsa.

Watt, Jean. Joint founder of SPON. She served on the Newport Beach City Council from 1988 to 1996.

Williams, Ray. Marine biology teacher at Rio Hondo College in Whittier with two master's degrees who manned the "Mud Stop" on Friends Tours. He was president of Friends of Newport Bay for three years, a Newport Bay Conservancy board member for 20 years, and a Newport Beach City Council member for four years.

Yeo, Ron. Architect of the Peter and Mary Muth Interpretive Center, Vista Point, and the Back Bay Science Center.

Zimmerman, Fern. Prominent lifetime member of the Sea & Sage Audubon Society, and co-founder of Friends of Newport Bay.

Newport Bay Presidents

Over the years the organization that protected Upper Newport Bay changed names several times. Friends of Newport Bay (FONB) was founded in 1967. Upper Newport Bay Naturalists (UNBN), which began in 1992, and the Friends of Newport Bay merged in 2000 and became Newport Bay Naturalists and Friends (NBNF). It was renamed Newport Bay Conservancy (NBC) in 2010, but the legal entity name remains Newport Bay Naturalists and Friends. Past presidents of these organizations are listed here:

Friends of Newport Bay (FONB)

1967 Chairman Jan Scherfig/Charles Greening

1968-1973 Charles Greening

1974-1976 Ray Williams

1977-1978 Records unavailable

1979 Ray Williams

1980 Charles Greening/Barton Ellerbroeck

1981-1984 Barton Ellerbroeck

1985-1987 John Roetman

1988-1999 Lane Koluvek

Upper Newport Bay Naturalists (UNBN)

1992 Lane Koluvek

1993-1999 Jack Keating

Newport Bay Naturalists and Friends (NBNF)

2000 Lane Koluvek

2001-2004 Jack Keating

2005 Gus Chabre

2006-2007 Regina Fodor

2008-2009 Dennis Baker

Newport Bay Conservancy (NBC)

2010 Blake Anderson

2011 Steve Bender

2012 Debbie Moore

2013-2014 Howard Cork

2015 Peter Fuhrer

2016-2018 Peter Bryant

2019 Randall English

Works Cited and Other Resources*

Newport Bay Conservancy archives, including *TRACKS* newsletters, Friends of Newport Bay letters, Orange County Foundation for the Preservation of Public Property letters, educational films, various personal letters and papers, and newspaper and magazine clippings.**

Frank and Frances Robinson Files on Upper Newport Bay Preservation. MS-R090. Special Collections and Archives, The UC Irvine Libraries, Irvine, California. Boxes 1, 2, 4, 6, 8, 15, 18, and 24 accessed November 30, 2016, December 8, 2016, April 13, 2017, October 19, 2018, January 23, 2019, July 19, 2019.

Aldridge, James A. (1998). *Saving the Bolsa Chica Wetlands,* The Amigos de Bolsa Chica, dissertation published by California State University, Fullerton, Center for Oral and Public History.

Brower, Martin A. (2013). *The Irvine Ranch: A Time for People.* Authorhouse.

Clarke, K. C. and Jeffrey J. Hemphill. (2002). *The Santa Barbara Oil Spill, A Retrospective.* Yearbook of the Association of Pacific Coast Geographers, Editor Darrick Danta, University of Hawai'i Press, vol. 64, pp. 157-162.

Personal interviews conducted 2017-2019 by Frances Cork, Annie Quinn, Chris Epting, and Cassandra Radcliff.

*Special thanks to Annie Quinn and Frances Cork for researching and organizing information.

**Archives also included articles from *Los Angeles Times, Orange County Register, Daily Pilot, Orange County Illustrated* magazine, *Fullerton Observer, Newport Harbor News Press, Irvine World News* (an Irvine Company publication), *Sunset Magazine, TIME* magazine, and *Electronics Group News.*

About Newport Bay Conservancy

Newport Bay Conservancy (NBC) bears a singular mission to protect and preserve the Upper Newport Bay and its watershed through education, restoration, research, and advocacy. For 50 years NBC has relied on the steady effort and dedication of members and volunteers without whom none of our aspirations and accomplishments, indeed our entire vision for the well-being and sustainability of the bay, would be possible. NBC continues to be the beneficiary of a strong tradition of volunteerism and a consistent history of community support.

About the Author and Author Acknowledgements

Cassandra Radcliff-Mendoza, a writer and editor from Orange County, California, began volunteering at Upper Newport Bay in 2014 after visiting the park for birdwatching. She currently lives in south Orange County with her husband and cat, and works for Walter Foster Publishing, a book publisher founded in Laguna Beach in 1922. Her passions are habitat restoration, local history, travel, and Disneyland. She thanks her husband, Pablo Mendoza, and her mother, Diane Radcliff, for attending volunteer events at the bay with her, for reading early drafts of this book, and for developing a passion for the Robinsons' story alongside her.

This project could not have been possible without the Keating family, Heather Cieslak, Frances and Howard Cork, Linda and Lane Koluvek, Annie Quinn, Teri Rider, Mary Thornton, and, of course, the heroes of Upper Newport Bay, Frank and Frances Robinson.